CLASSIC
RECIPES

Publications
International Ltd.

Favorite Brand Name Recipes at www.fbnr.com

Special thanks to the Campbell's Kitchen, Lucinda Ayers, Vice President, and Catherine Marschean-Spivak, Group Manager.

Photography on pages 31, 32, 39, 45, 49, 55, 56, 59, 61, 63, 66, 73, 88, 95, 97, 101, 108, 113, 114, 120, 121 and 123 by Stephen Hamilton Photographics, Inc., Chicago.

Pictured on the front cover: Green Bean Casserole (*page 105*).
Pictured on the back cover (clockwise from top): Pork Chop Skillet Dinner (*page 72*), Swiss Vegetable Bake (*page 112*), Tomato Soup Spice Cake (*page 123*) and Cheesy Chicken and Rice Bake (*page 33*).

ISBN-13: 978-1-4127-2462-3
ISBN-10: 1-4127-2462-7

Manufactured in China.

8 7 6 5 4 3 2 1

Microwave Cooking: Microwave ovens vary in wattage. Use the cooking times as guidelines and check for doneness before adding more time.

Preparation/Cooking Times: Preparation times are based on the approximate amount of time required to assemble the recipe before cooking, baking, chilling or serving. These times include preparation steps such as measuring, chopping and mixing. The fact that some preparations and cooking can be done simultaneously is taken into account. Preparation of optional ingredients and serving suggestions is not included.

Contents

Welcome to Campbell's®
Classic Recipes

When John T. Dorrance bought the Joseph Campbell Company in 1915, he probably had no idea that people would use soup as a recipe ingredient. His goal at the time was just to convince Americans that they should be eating more soup. So, in 1910, when the first cookbook was published—a booklet, really, called *Campbell's Menu Book*—it was based on a month's worth of menus that focused on soup as the integral part of the meal: soup for lunch, soup for dinner, plus suggested appetizers and entrées that would complement the soup, rather than the other way around.

Some years later, when Dorrance realized that American cooks weren't just eating soup, they were also using it as sauce, the next cookbook, *Helps for the Hostess*, published in 1916, showcased soup as sauce and gravy. Tomato Soup, for instance, was to be thickened with a roux and seasoned before serving it over a vegetable loaf. In 1941, *Easy Ways to Good Meals* listed menus that not only used soup as one of the courses, but also used soup as an important ingredient in the recipes. "So," the book stated, "here are soups with not just one use, but dozens!"

Over the years, the Campbell Soup Company has published many cookbooks. It is fascinating to study the evolution of our cookbooks and the evolution of American cooking from these books: We recently did just that as we planned this cookbook you now hold in your hands, and realized through all the changes—from the precious, dainty luncheons and seriously formal dinners of the early 1900s that featured soup as the focal point of the meal, to today's fun lunch of soup garnished with Goldfish® crackers for the kids and a casual family casserole supper—Campbell Soup Company has continued to address the changing recipe needs of the American family.

Offering ways to use our foods in family-pleasing recipes is an important mission for us. We have learned that the more things change, the more they stay the same. Take Tuna Noodle Casserole, for instance, one of Campbell's popular casserole recipes. It was developed in the late 1950s. The original recipe called for Campbell's® Condensed Cream of Celery Soup and was topped with crushed potato chips, a popular taste combination then. As families developed different taste preferences, the recipe was changed to introduce Campbell's® Condensed Cream of Mushroom Soup and breadcrumb topping. The casserole is still made with Campbell's® Condensed Cream of Mushroom Soup, but today's family prefers cheese topping, so the recipe on page 38 features melted Cheddar cheese on top.

We consider Tuna Noodle Casserole to be one of our classic recipes. But what defines a classic? According to the dictionary, a "classic" is something that serves as a standard of excellence, something enduring, something traditional, something tried and true. Our classic recipes are traditions that one generation of cooks has handed down to the next, so many Americans have grown up with these recipes. But with growth comes change, and just as the culinary demands of American families keep changing, our recipes change to keep up with them.

Families still want recipes like Tuna Noodle Casserole even more than 50 years after it was introduced. Likewise, many of us can't imagine a holiday dinner table without Green Bean Casserole or a week without Best Ever Meatloaf. We in Campbell's Kitchen know our classic recipes—as well as our new recipes—are an important and helpful part of your life. And we hope that, by continuing to listen to you and updating recipes as your needs and tastes change, our classics will continue to be the tried and true recipes you have come to rely on for easy, delicious meals that your family loves.

Throughout this book, in addition to our classic recipes, we also provide helpful tips, fascinating insights we hope you'll find interesting and a little history of our company and our recipes. We hope *Classic Recipes* will become an essential part of your kitchen, and that, when the time comes, you can hand these recipes down to the next generation of cooks in your family.

FAVORITE
30-MINUTE
MEALS

American families have never been busier, and we're sure yours is no exception. These days, we all need meals we can get on the table fast. Campbell's Kitchen comes to your rescue with these dishes—all go from stove to table in no more than half an hour.

Tasty 2-Step Chicken

PREP/COOK: 20 MINUTES

1 tablespoon vegetable oil
4 skinless, boneless chicken breast halves
1 can (10¾ ounces) Campbell's® Condensed Cream of Mushroom Soup (Regular **or** 98% Fat Free)
½ cup water

1. Heat the oil in a 10-inch skillet over medium-high heat. Add the chicken and cook for 10 minutes or until it's well browned on both sides. Remove the chicken and set aside. Pour off any fat.

2. Stir the soup and water into the skillet. Heat to a boil. Return the chicken to the skillet and reduce the heat to low. Cover and cook for 5 minutes or until the chicken is cooked through.

Makes 4 servings

Tried
& True: *It began life in 1962 as Glori-fried Chicken: lightly browned cut-up chicken placed in a baking dish, covered with cream soup and baked or cooked on the top of the stove. In the 1980s, it was renamed Souper Baked Chicken and was prepared in the oven. Now it's called Tasty 2-Step Chicken, prepared like Glori-fried Chicken but using today's cook's preference: boneless, skinless chicken breasts.*

PREP: 5 MINUTES
COOK: 15 MINUTES

Did you know…?
Pace was the first prepared salsa sold in the United States—in 1947. We pride ourselves on its fresh-tasting ingredients and made-in-Texas stature. Although most salsa is used for dipping, the second most popular use is at breakfast.

Monterey Chicken Fajitas

2	tablespoons vegetable oil
4	skinless, boneless chicken breasts, cut into strips
1	medium green pepper, cut into 2-inch long strips (about 1½ cups)
1	medium onion, sliced (about ½ cup)
1	can (10¾ ounces) Campbell's® Condensed Cream of Mushroom Soup (Regular **or** 98% Fat Free)
½	cup Pace® Chunky Salsa
8	flour tortillas (8-inch), warmed
1	cup shredded Monterey Jack cheese (4 ounces)

1. Heat the oil in a 10-inch skillet over medium-high heat. Add the chicken and cook until it's well browned, stirring often.

2. Reduce the heat to medium. Add the pepper and onion. Cook and stir until the vegetables are tender-crisp.

3. Stir the soup and salsa into the skillet. Cook until the chicken is cooked through.

4. Spoon **about ½ cup** of the chicken mixture down the center of each tortilla. Top with the cheese and additional salsa. Fold the tortilla around the filling.

Makes 8 fajitas

PREP: 5 MINUTES
COOK: 15 MINUTES

Did you know…?

Stir-fries began to
appear in Campbell's
cookbooks in the 1970s.
Soy sauce is almost
always an ingredient. Soy
sauce comes in several
varieties: regular and
low-sodium, flavored,
such as mushroom and
light and dark, which
refer to both the color
and depth of flavor.

Asian Chicken Stir-Fry

1   tablespoon vegetable oil
1   pound skinless, boneless chicken breasts, cut into strips
1   can (10¾ ounces) Campbell's® Condensed Golden
      Mushroom Soup
2   tablespoons soy sauce
1   teaspoon garlic powder
1   bag (16 ounces) any frozen vegetable combination
      Hot cooked rice

1. Heat the oil in a 10-inch skillet over medium-high heat. Add the
chicken and stir-fry until it's well browned.

2. Stir the soup, soy sauce and garlic powder into the skillet. Heat to a
boil. Add the vegetables. Cook and stir until the vegetables are tender-
crisp. Serve over the rice.

Makes 4 servings

PREP/COOK: 25 MINUTES

Did you know…?
Campbell Soup Company purchased C.A. Swanson & Sons in 1955. Swanson was a canning and frozen foods company in Omaha, Nebraska, started by a 20-year-old Swedish immigrant. His sons took over the company upon his death and went on to create the TV dinner. (Campbell Soup Company sold the frozen food division in 1998.)

25-Minute Chicken & Noodles

1¾ cups Swanson® Chicken Broth (Regular, Natural Goodness™
        or Certified Organic)
½   teaspoon dried basil leaves, crushed
⅛   teaspoon ground black pepper
2   cups frozen vegetable combination (broccoli, cauliflower,
        carrots)
2   cups **uncooked** medium egg noodles
2   cups cubed cooked chicken

1. Heat the broth, basil, black pepper and vegetables in a 10-inch skillet over high heat to a boil. Reduce the heat to low. Cover and cook for 5 minutes.

2. Stir the noodles into the skillet. Cover and cook for 5 minutes more. Add the chicken. Cook and stir until hot.

Makes 4 servings

PREP/COOK: 20 MINUTES

Chicken Creole
with Chile Cream Sauce

4 skinless, boneless chicken breast halves
2 teaspoons Creole **or** Cajun seasoning
1 tablespoon olive oil
1 can (10¾ ounces) Campbell's® Condensed Cream of
   Chicken Soup (Regular **or** 98% Fat Free)
½ cup water
1 can (4 ounces) chopped green chiles
1 teaspoon lime juice
¼ cup sour cream
   Hot cooked rice with peas

1. Season the chicken with the Creole seasoning.

2. Heat the oil in a 10-inch skillet over medium-high heat. Add the chicken and cook until it's well browned on both sides. Remove the chicken and set aside.

3. Stir the soup, water, chiles and lime juice into the skillet. Heat to a boil. Return the chicken to the skillet and reduce the heat to low. Cover and cook for 5 minutes or until the chicken is cooked through.

4. Stir in the sour cream. Cook and stir until hot. Serve with the rice.

Makes 4 servings

PREP: 5 MINUTES
COOK: 25 MINUTES

Easy Chicken and Pasta

- 1 tablespoon vegetable oil
- 4 skinless, boneless chicken breasts, cut into 1-inch pieces
- 1 can (10¾ ounces) Campbell's® Condensed Cream of Mushroom Soup (Regular **or** 98% Fat Free)
- 2¼ cups water
- ½ teaspoon dried basil leaves, crushed
- 2 cups frozen vegetable combination (broccoli, cauliflower, carrots)
- 2 cups **uncooked** corkscrew-shaped pasta (rotini)
  Grated Parmesan cheese

1. Heat the oil in a 10-inch skillet over medium-high heat. Add the chicken and cook until it's well browned, stirring often. Remove the chicken with a slotted spoon and set aside.

2. Stir the soup, water, basil and vegetables into the skillet. Heat to a boil. Add the pasta. Reduce the heat to medium. Cook and stir for 10 minutes.

3. Return the chicken to the skillet. Cook for 5 minutes more or until the pasta is tender but still firm. Sprinkle with the cheese.

Makes 4 servings

Italian Herbed Chicken & Penne Pasta

PREP/COOK: 25 MINUTES

1¾ cups Swanson® Chicken Broth (Regular, Natural Goodness™ **or** Certified Organic)
6 sun-dried tomatoes
1 tablespoon olive oil
4 skinless, boneless chicken breasts, cut into strips
2 cups sliced mushrooms
½ teaspoon minced fresh garlic
1 tablespoon all-purpose flour
½ teaspoon Italian seasoning, crushed
1 cup packed coarsely chopped fresh spinach
3 cups tube-shaped pasta (penne), cooked and drained
Grated Parmesan cheese

Easy Substitution Tip:
Substitute 3 plum tomatoes, chopped, for the sun-dried tomatoes. Add with spinach and pasta.

Did you know…?
Sun-dried tomatoes are available dried, usually in plastic packages in the produce section of the supermarket, or dried and then packed in oil in jars or bottles. For this recipe, use the dried variety not packed in oil.

1. Put the broth and tomatoes in a microwavable measuring cup. Microwave on HIGH for 2 minutes. Let stand for 5 minutes. Remove the tomatoes and cut up. Reserve the broth.

2. Heat the oil in a nonstick 12-inch skillet. Add the chicken and cook until it's well browned, stirring often.

3. Add the mushrooms and garlic and cook until tender. Stir in the flour and Italian seasoning. Cook and stir for 1 minute more.

4. Stir the tomatoes and broth into the skillet. Cook and stir until the mixture boils and thickens. Stir in the spinach and pasta. Serve with the cheese.

Makes 4 servings

PREP: 5 MINUTES
COOK: 20 MINUTES

Paprika Chicken
with Sour Cream Gravy

½ cup all-purpose flour

2 teaspoons paprika

1 teaspoon **each** garlic powder, ground black pepper **and** ground red pepper

4 skinless, boneless chicken breast halves

4 tablespoons butter

1 can (10¾ ounces) Campbell's® Condensed Cream of Chicken Soup (Regular **or** 98% Fat Free)

2 medium green onions, sliced (about ¼ cup)

1 container (8 ounces) sour cream

1. Mix the flour, paprika, garlic powder, black pepper and red pepper on a plate. Coat the chicken with the flour mixture.

2. Heat the butter in a 10-inch skillet over medium-high heat. Add the chicken and cook for 10 minutes or until it's well browned on both sides. Remove the chicken and set aside.

3. Stir the soup and green onions into the skillet. Heat to a boil. Return the chicken to the skillet and reduce the heat to low. Cover and cook for 10 minutes or until the chicken is cooked through. Stir in the sour cream.

Makes 4 servings

PREP: 10 MINUTES
COOK: 15 MINUTES

Chicken & Broccoli Alfredo

½ of a 12 ounce package fettuccine pasta, cooked and drained
1 cup fresh **or** frozen broccoli flowerets
2 tablespoons butter
1 pound skinless, boneless chicken breasts, cut into 1-inch pieces
1 can (10¾ ounces) Campbell's® Condensed Cream of Mushroom Soup (Regular **or** 98% Fat Free)
½ cup milk
½ cup grated Parmesan cheese
¼ teaspoon freshly ground black pepper

1. Prepare the pasta according to the package directions in a 3-quart saucepan. Add the broccoli during the last 4 minutes of the cooking time. Drain the pasta and broccoli well in a colander and return them to the saucepan.

2. Heat the butter in a 10-inch skillet over medium-high heat. Add the chicken and cook until it's well browned, stirring often.

3. Stir the soup, milk, cheese, black pepper and pasta mixture into the skillet. Cook and stir until the mixture is hot and bubbling.

Makes 4 servings

Chicken Noodle Soup Express

2 cans (10½ ounces **each**) Campbell's® Condensed Chicken Broth
1 cup water
  Generous dash ground black pepper
1 medium carrot, sliced (about ½ cup)
1 stalk celery, sliced (about ½ cup)
2 skinless, boneless chicken breasts, cut into cubes
½ cup **uncooked** medium egg noodles

1. Heat the broth, water, black pepper, carrot, celery and chicken in a 2-quart saucepan over high heat to a boil.

2. Stir the noodles into the saucepan. Reduce the heat to medium. Cook for 10 minutes or until the noodles are tender but still firm, stirring occasionally.

Makes 4 servings

20-Minute Herbed Chicken

PREP/COOK: 20 MINUTES

1 tablespoon vegetable oil
4 skinless, boneless chicken breast halves
1 can (10¾ ounces) Campbell's® Condensed Cream of Chicken with Herbs Soup
½ cup milk
Broth Simmered Rice (recipe on page 106)

1. Heat the oil in a 10-inch skillet over medium-high heat. Add the chicken and cook for 10 minutes or until it's well browned on both sides. Remove the chicken and set aside.

2. Stir the soup and milk into the skillet. Heat to a boil. Return the chicken to the skillet and reduce the heat to low. Cover and cook for 5 minutes or until the chicken is cooked through. Serve with Broth Simmered Rice.

Makes 4 servings

PREP: 5 MINUTES
COOK: 20 MINUTES

Easy Beef & Pasta

    1   tablespoon vegetable oil
    1   pound boneless beef sirloin **or** top round steak, ¾-inch thick,
          cut into thin strips
    1   can (10¾ ounces) Campbell's® Condensed Tomato Soup
          (Regular **or** Healthy Request®)
    ½   cup water
    1   bag (about 16 ounces) frozen vegetable and pasta blend

1. Heat the oil in a 10-inch skillet over medium-high heat. Add the beef and cook until it's well browned, stirring often.

2. Stir the soup, water and vegetable pasta blend into the skillet. Heat to a boil. Reduce the heat to low. Cover and cook for 5 minutes or until the pasta is tender but still firm.

Makes 4 servings

French Onion Burgers

1   pound ground beef
1   can (10½ ounces) Campbell's® Condensed French Onion Soup
4   slices cheese
4   round hard rolls, split

1. Shape the beef into 4 (½-inch thick) burgers.

2. Heat a 10-inch skillet over medium-high heat. Add the burgers and cook until they're well browned on both sides. Remove the burgers and set aside. Pour off any fat.

3. Stir in the soup. Heat to a boil. Return the burgers to the skillet and reduce the heat to low. Cover and cook for 5 minutes or until the burgers are cooked through. Top with cheese and continue cooking until the cheese melts. Serve burgers in rolls with soup mixture for dipping.

Makes 4 burgers

PREP/COOK: 20 MINUTES

20-Minute Seafood Stew

Tip:

Try any one or a combination of the following: Firm white fish fillets (cut into 2-inch pieces), boneless fish steaks (cut into 1-inch cubes), medium shrimp (shelled and deveined) or scallops.

2   cups Prego® Traditional Italian Sauce
1   bottle (8 fluid ounces) clam juice
¼   cup Burgundy **or** other dry red wine (optional)
1   pound fresh fish **and/or** shellfish
8   small clams in shells, well scrubbed*
    Chopped fresh parsley

Before cooking, discard any clams that remain open when tapped.

1. Mix the Italian sauce, clam juice and wine in a 3-quart saucepan over high heat to a boil. Reduce the heat to low. Cook for 5 minutes.

2. Add the fish and clams to the saucepan. Cover and cook for 5 minutes or until the fish flakes easily when tested with a fork and the clams are open. Discard any clams that do not open. Sprinkle with the parsley.

Makes 4 servings

Seafood Tomato Alfredo

PREP: 5 MINUTES
COOK: 20 MINUTES

1   tablespoon butter
1   medium onion, chopped (about ½ cup)
1   can (10¾ ounces) Campbell's® Condensed Cream of
       Mushroom with Roasted Garlic Soup
½   cup milk
1   cup diced canned tomatoes
1   pound fresh fish fillets (flounder, haddock **or** halibut), cut into
       2-inch pieces
       Hot cooked linguine

1. Heat the butter in a 10-inch skillet over medium heat. Add the onion and cook until it's tender.

2. Stir the soup, milk and tomatoes into the skillet. Heat to a boil. Add the fish to the skillet and reduce the heat to low. Cover and cook for 10 minutes or until the fish flakes easily when tested with a fork.

3. Serve over the linguine.

Makes 4 servings

Did you know…?
You can use any of Campbell's condensed cream soups as white sauces. Campbell's® Condensed Cream of Mushroom Soup, created in 1934, was widely used as a sauce, and because of its convenience and versatility—and good taste—radically changed the way America cooked.

PREP/COOK: 20 MINUTES

Polynesian Pork Chops

4 boneless pork chops, ¾-inch thick
1 teaspoon garlic powder
1 tablespoon vegetable oil
1 medium onion, chopped (about ½ cup)
1 can (10¾ ounces) Campbell's® Condensed Golden Mushroom Soup
¼ cup water
1 can (8 ounces) pineapple chunks, undrained
3 tablespoons soy sauce
1 tablespoon honey
Hot cooked rice
Sliced green onions

1. Season the chops with the garlic powder.

2. Heat the oil in a 10-inch skillet over medium-high heat. Add the pork chops and cook until the chops are well browned on both sides. Add the onion.

3. Stir the soup, water, pineapple with juice, soy sauce and honey into the skillet. Heat to a boil. Reduce the heat to low. Cover and cook for 10 minutes or until the chops are cooked through but slightly pink in center.

4. Serve with the rice and sprinkle with the green onions.

Makes 4 servings

Tried & True: *When Campbell's Kitchen held its 20-Minute Recipe Challenge in 1999, the winner got her picture on the label of Campbell's Condensed Golden Mushroom Soup cans for a year. The winning recipe? Polynesian Pork Chops. Since then, it's been one of Campbell's very popular recipes.*

PREP/COOK: 20 MINUTES

Saucy Pork Chops

1 tablespoon vegetable oil

4 bone-in pork chops, ½-inch thick

1 can (10¾ ounces) Campbell's® Condensed Cream of
   Onion Soup

¼ cup water

Did you know…?

Pork no longer has to be cooked until it's white to be safe. Today's pork is perfectly safe when it's cooked until it's just a little pink in the center, 160°F.

1. Heat the oil in a 10-inch skillet over medium-high heat. Add the pork chops and cook until the chops are well browned on both sides.

2. Stir the soup and water into the skillet. Heat to a boil. Reduce the heat to low. Cover and cook for 10 minutes or until the chops are cooked through but slightly pink in center.

Makes 4 servings

Simple Salisbury Steak

PREP: 5 MINUTES
COOK: 25 MINUTES

- 1 pound ground beef
- 1 can (10¾ ounces) Campbell's® Condensed Cream of Mushroom Soup (Regular **or** 98% Fat Free)
- ⅓ cup dry breadcrumbs
- 1 egg, beaten
- 1 small onion, finely chopped (about ¼ cup)
- 1 tablespoon vegetable oil
- 1½ cups sliced mushrooms

1. Thoroughly mix the beef, **¼ cup** of the soup, breadcrumbs, egg and onion in a medium bowl. Shape the mixture into 4 (½-inch thick) burgers.

2. Heat the oil in a 10-inch skillet over medium-high heat. Add the burgers and cook until well browned on both sides. Remove the burgers with a slotted spatula and set aside.

3. Stir the remaining soup and mushrooms into the skillet. Heat to a boil. Return the burgers to the skillet and reduce the heat to low. Cover and cook for 10 minutes or until the burgers are cooked through.

Makes 4 servings

Did you know...?
Making breadcrumbs is easy. For dry breadcrumbs, preheat your oven to 300°F. Place a single layer of bread slices on a baking sheet; bake 5 to 8 minutes or until they're completely dry and lightly browned. Cool completely. Process in a food processor or crush or crumble in a plastic food storage bag until crumbs are very fine. Season as desired.

ONE-DISH AND CASSEROLE DINNERS

Campbell's Kitchen didn't *really* invent the casserole, of course, but we like to think Campbell's® condensed cream soups—such as Cream of Mushroom, Cream of Celery, Cream of Asparagus and others—had something to do with their incredible popularity and staying power. Casseroles are high on the list of America's favorite home-cooked meals, and here you'll find our time-tested, taste-tested one-dish favorites.

Cheesy Chicken and Rice Bake

PREP: 5 MINUTES
BAKE: 45 MINUTES

- 1 can (10¾ ounces) Campbell's® Condensed Cream of Chicken Soup (Regular **or** 98% Fat Free)
- 1⅓ cups water
- ¾ cup **uncooked** regular long-grain white rice
- ½ teaspoon onion powder
- ¼ teaspoon ground black pepper
- 4 to 6 skinless, boneless chicken breast halves
- 1 cup shredded Cheddar cheese (4 ounces)

Tip:

Stir 2 cups of fresh, canned or frozen vegetables into the soup mixture before topping with chicken.

1. Stir the soup, water, rice, onion powder and black pepper in a 12×8×2-inch shallow baking dish. Top with the chicken. Sprinkle the chicken with additional pepper. Cover the dish with foil.

2. Bake at 375°F. for 45 minutes or until the chicken is cooked through and the rice is tender and most of the liquid is absorbed.

3. Uncover and sprinkle the cheese over the chicken.

Makes 6 servings

Tried & True: *Cheesy Chicken and Rice Bake—a variation of a 1995 recipe, One-Dish Chicken and Rice Bake—is one of the first examples of what we call the "new" casserole: Uncooked ingredients are layered in a pan or skillet and baked or cooked on the top of the stove. In this recipe, rice, Campbell's Condensed Cream of Chicken Soup and water are stirred together in a baking dish. Chicken pieces are placed on top and are seasoned with onion powder and ground black pepper, and then baked. Using uncooked ingredients saves the cook more time and makes a quick recipe even easier.*

PREP: 20 MINUTES
BAKE: 20 MINUTES

Baked Macaroni & Cheese

1   can (10¾ ounces) Campbell's® Condensed Cheddar
      Cheese Soup

½   soup can milk

⅛   teaspoon ground black pepper

1½   cups corkscrew-shaped pasta (rotini) **or** medium shell-shaped
      pasta, cooked and drained

1   tablespoon dry bread crumbs

2   teaspoons butter, melted

1. Stir the soup, milk, black pepper and pasta in a 1-quart casserole.

2. Mix the bread crumbs with the butter in a small cup. Sprinkle over the pasta mixture.

3. Bake at 400°F. for 20 minutes or until hot.

Makes 4 servings

Baked Pork Chops with Apple Raisin Stuffing

PREP: 15 MINUTES
BAKE: 35 MINUTES

- 1   cup applesauce
- ½   cup water
- 2   tablespoons butter, melted
- 1   stalk celery, chopped (about ½ cup)
- 2   tablespoons raisins
- 4   cups Pepperidge Farm® Herb Seasoned Stuffing
- 4   boneless pork chops, ¾-inch thick
     Paprika **or** ground cinnamon
     Apple slices (optional)

1. Stir the applesauce, water, butter, celery and raisins in a medium bowl. Add the stuffing and stir lightly to coat. Spoon the stuffing mixture into a 12×8×2-inch shallow baking dish. Arrange the pork chops over the stuffing. Sprinkle paprika over the chops.

2. Bake at 400°F. for 35 minutes or until the chops are cooked through but slightly pink in center. Top with apple slices, if desired.

Makes 4 servings

PREP: 10 MINUTES
BAKE: 30 MINUTES

Beef Taco Bake

1 pound ground beef

1 can (10¾ ounces) Campbell's® Condensed Tomato Soup (Regular **or** Healthy Request®)

1 cup Pace® Chunky Salsa **or** Picante Sauce

½ cup milk

6 (8-inch) flour tortillas **or** 8 (6-inch) corn tortillas, cut into 1-inch pieces

1 cup shredded Cheddar cheese (4 ounces)

1. Cook the beef in a 10-inch skillet over medium-high heat until the beef is well browned, stirring frequently to break up meat. Pour off any fat.

2. Stir the soup, salsa, milk, tortillas and **½ cup** of the cheese into the skillet. Spoon into a 12×8×2-inch shallow baking dish. Cover the dish with foil.

3. Bake at 400°F. for 30 minutes or until hot. Sprinkle with the remaining cheese.

Makes 4 servings

Chicken Broccoli Divan

PREP: 10 MINUTES
BAKE: 45 MINUTES

8 cups fresh **or** frozen broccoli flowerets

8 skinless, boneless chicken breast halves

1 can (26 ounces) Campbell's® Condensed Cream
    of Chicken Soup

1¼ cups milk

1 cup shredded Cheddar cheese (4 ounces)

¼ cup dry bread crumbs

2 tablespoons butter, melted

Did you know…?
Boneless chicken breasts don't require as much cooking time as bone-in chicken breasts, making them even more convenient.

1. Place the broccoli in a 4-quart shallow baking dish. Top with the chicken.

2. Stir the soup and milk with a whisk or spoon in a medium bowl. Pour the soup mixture over the chicken. Sprinkle with the cheese.

3. Mix the bread crumbs with the butter in a small cup. Sprinkle over the cheese.

4. Bake at 350°F. for 45 minutes or until the chicken is cooked through.

Makes 8 servings

PREP: 10 MINUTES
BAKE: 22 MINUTES

Easy Substitution Tip:
Substitute your family's favorite frozen vegetable for the peas.

Tuna Noodle Casserole

1　can (10¾ ounces) Campbell's® Condensed Cream of Mushroom
　　Soup (Regular **or** 98% Fat Free)
½　cup milk
1　cup frozen peas
2　cans (about 6 ounces **each**) tuna, drained and flaked
2　cups hot cooked medium egg noodles
½　cup shredded Cheddar cheese

1. Stir the soup, milk, peas, tuna and noodles in a 1½-quart casserole.

2. Bake at 400°F. for 20 minutes or until hot. Stir.

3. Sprinkle cheese over the tuna mixture. Bake for 2 minutes more or until the cheese melts.

Makes 4 servings

Tried & True: *This popular casserole from Campbell's Kitchen was developed in the late 1950s and is the perfect example of what a Campbell Soup Company recipe strives to be: easy to prepare and using a minimum of ingredients while offering great flavors with wide appeal. The original recipe called for Campbell's® Condensed Cream of Celery Soup and was topped with crushed potato chips. Over the years, Campbell's Kitchen has substituted Campbell's Condensed Cream of Mushroom Soup for the original Condensed Cream of Celery Soup and breadcrumbs for the original potato chips. Today the recipe is still made with Condensed Cream of Mushroom Soup, but is often topped with Cheddar cheese.*

PREP/COOK: 15 MINUTES

Classic Campbelled Eggs

1 can (10¾ ounces) Campbell's® Condensed Cream of Celery Soup (Regular **or** 98% Fat Free)

8 eggs, beaten
   Dash ground black pepper

2 tablespoons butter
   Chopped fresh parsley **or** chives

1. Beat the soup, eggs and black pepper with a whisk in a large bowl.

2. Heat the butter in a 12-inch skillet over medium heat. Add the egg mixture. Cook until the eggs are set but still very moist, stirring lightly. Sprinkle with the parsley.

Makes 4 servings

Tried & True: A brunch favorite, Classic Campbelled Eggs was developed in the 1960s and could be one of our easiest recipes. The recipe can be made with any of the Campbell's® condensed cream soups—Cream of Celery, Cream of Potato, Cream of Mushroom or Cream of Chicken—or with Condensed Cheddar Cheese Soup. Just beat 8 eggs into a bowl with a can of your chosen soup, season with ground black pepper and scramble just until the eggs are set. The recipe has appeared in advertising, on the soup can label, in cookbooks—even in an ad in Field and Stream, *the fishing and hunting magazine, to appeal to those who are looking for an easy breakfast recipe to cook outdoors!*

Chicken with White Beans

PREP: 5 MINUTES
COOK: 45 MINUTES

1   tablespoon vegetable oil
4   bone-in chicken breast halves*
2   cups Prego® Traditional Italian Sauce
¼   teaspoon garlic powder **or** 2 cloves garlic, minced
1   large onion, chopped (about 1 cup)
2   cans (about 15 ounces **each**) white kidney (cannellini) beans,
     rinsed and drained

If desired, remove skin from the chicken before browning.

1. Heat the oil in a 10-inch skillet over medium-high heat. Add the chicken and cook for 10 minutes or until it's well browned on both sides. Remove the chicken and set aside.

2. Stir the Italian sauce, garlic powder, onion and beans into the skillet. Heat to a boil. Return the chicken to the skillet. Reduce the heat to low. Cover and cook for 30 minutes or until the chicken is cooked through.

Makes 4 servings

PREP: 10 MINUTES
BAKE: 25 MINUTES

Country Chicken Casserole

1   can (10¾ ounces) Campbell's® Condensed Cream of Celery Soup (Regular **or** 98% Fat Free)

1   can (10¾ ounces) Campbell's® Condensed Cream of Potato Soup

1   cup milk

¼   teaspoon dried thyme leaves, crushed

⅛   teaspoon ground black pepper

4   cups cooked cut up vegetables*

2   cups cubed cooked chicken **or** turkey

1½   cups water

4   tablespoons butter

4   cups Pepperidge Farm® Herb Seasoned Stuffing

Use a combination of cut green beans and sliced carrots.

1. Stir the soups, milk, thyme, black pepper, vegetables and chicken in a 13×9×2-inch shallow baking dish.

2. Heat the water and butter in 2-quart saucepan over high heat to a boil. Add the stuffing and stir lightly to coat. Spoon the stuffing over the chicken mixture.

3. Bake at 400°F. for 25 minutes or until hot.

Makes 5 servings

PREP: 10 MINUTES
BAKE: 1 HOUR
STAND: 5 MINUTES

Time-Saving Tip:

To thaw spinach, microwave on HIGH for 3 minutes, breaking apart with a fork halfway through heating.

Chicken Florentine Lasagna

2 cans (10¾ ounces **each**) Campbell's® Condensed Cream of Chicken with Herbs Soup

2 cups milk

1 egg

1 container (15 ounces) ricotta cheese

6 **uncooked** lasagna noodles

1 package (about 10 ounces) frozen chopped spinach, thawed and well drained

2 cups cubed cooked chicken **or** turkey

2 cups shredded Cheddar cheese (8 ounces)

1. Stir the soup and milk with a whisk or spoon in a medium bowl.

2. Stir the egg and ricotta cheese in a small bowl.

3. Spread **1 cup** of the soup mixture in a 13×9×2-inch shallow baking dish. Top with **3** of the lasagna noodles, ricotta mixture, spinach, chicken, **1 cup** of the Cheddar cheese and **1 cup** of the soup mixture. Top with remaining lasagna noodles and remaining soup mixture. Cover the dish with foil.

4. Bake at 375°F. for 1 hour. Uncover and top with remaining Cheddar cheese. Let the lasagna stand for 5 minutes before serving.

Makes 6 servings

PREP: 15 MINUTES
BAKE: 40 MINUTES

Did you know…?

You can have a chicken casserole at a moment's notice if you have cooked chicken on hand. Buy boneless chicken breasts, cut them into bite-size pieces and stir-fry in a little vegetable or olive oil in a skillet over medium heat until they're no longer pink in the center. Drain off the fat, and package them in 1- and 2-cup amounts in sealable plastic freezer bags. Freeze. Thaw in the refrigerator or in the microwave, and use according to recipe directions.

King Ranch Casserole

 1 can (10¾ ounces) Campbell's® Condensed Cream of Mushroom Soup (Regular **or** 98% Fat Free)
 ¾ cup Pace® Picante Sauce
 ¾ cup sour cream
 1 tablespoon chili powder
 2 medium tomatoes, chopped (about 2 cups)
 3 cups cubed cooked chicken **or** turkey
 12 corn tortillas (6-inch), cut into 1-inch pieces
 1 cup shredded Cheddar cheese (4 ounces)
    Sliced green onions

1. Stir the soup, picante sauce, sour cream, chili powder, tomatoes and chicken in a large bowl.

2. Place **half** of the tortillas in a 12×8×2-inch shallow baking dish. Top with **half** the chicken mixture. Repeat the layers. Sprinkle with the cheese.

3. Bake at 350°F. for 40 minutes or until hot. Serve with additional picante sauce and sour cream. Sprinkle with green onions.

Makes 8 servings

Pork with Roasted Peppers & Potatoes

PREP/COOK: 25 MINUTES

Did you know…?
Roasted bell peppers are available in jars, or you can roast them over a gas burner, on the grill, or under the broiler. Cook whole peppers until they are charred and blistered all over. Put them in a plastic or paper bag, seal and let stand for about 10 minutes. Peel or rub the charred skin off and chop the pepper.

4   boneless pork chops, ½-inch thick
    Ground black pepper
1   tablespoon olive oil
4   medium red potatoes, (about 1 pound), cut into 1-inch pieces
1   medium onion, sliced (about ½ cup)
1   teaspoon dried oregano leaves, crushed
1   cup Swanson® Chicken Broth (Regular, Natural Goodness™ **or** Certified Organic)
½   cup diced roasted sweet peppers

1. Season the chops with black pepper.

2. Heat the oil in a 10-inch nonstick skillet over medium-high heat. Add the pork chops and cook until well browned on both sides. Remove the chops and set aside.

3. Add the potatoes, onion and oregano to the skillet. Cook and stir for 5 minutes or until browned.

4. Stir the broth and sweet peppers into the skillet. Heat to a boil. Return the chops to the skillet and reduce the heat to low. Cover and cook for 10 minutes or until the chops are cooked through but slightly pink in center.

Makes 4 servings

47

PREP/BAKE: 30 MINUTES

Time-Saving Tip:
To thaw vegetables,
microwave on HIGH
for 3 minutes.

Garlic Mashed Potatoes & Beef Bake

1 pound ground beef **or** ground turkey

1 can (10¾ ounces) Campbell's® Condensed Cream of Mushroom with Roasted Garlic Soup

1 tablespoon Worcestershire sauce

1 bag (16 ounces) frozen vegetables combination (broccoli, cauliflower, carrots), thawed

2 cups water

3 tablespoons butter

¾ cup milk

2 cups instant potato flakes **or** buds

1. Cook the beef in a 10-inch skillet over medium-high heat until the beef is well browned, stirring frequently to break up meat. Pour off any fat.

2. Stir the beef, **½ can** of the soup, Worcestershire and vegetables in a 12×8×2-inch shallow baking dish.

3. Heat the water, butter and remaining soup in a 2-quart saucepan over high heat to a boil. Remove from the heat. Stir in the milk. Slowly stir in the potatoes. Spoon potatoes over the beef mixture.

4. Bake at 400°F. for 20 minutes or until hot.

Makes 4 servings

PREP: 10 MINUTES
COOK: 30 MINUTES

Chicken Cacciatore & Pasta

    1   tablespoon vegetable oil
    4   skinless, boneless chicken breast halves **or** 8 boneless chicken
         thighs, skin removed
 1¾   cups Swanson® Chicken Broth (Regular, Natural Goodness™
         or Certified Organic)
    1   teaspoon dried oregano leaves, crushed
    ½   teaspoon garlic powder
    1   can (14 ounces) whole peeled tomatoes, cut up
    1   small green pepper, cut into 2-inch long strips (about 1 cup)
    1   medium onion, cut into wedges
 2½   cups **uncooked** shell-shaped pasta (medium shells)

1. Heat the oil in a 10-inch skillet over medium-high heat. Add the
chicken and cook for 10 minutes or until it's well browned on both sides.
Remove the chicken and set aside.

2. Stir the broth, oregano, garlic powder, tomatoes, pepper and onion
into the skillet. Heat to a boil. Stir in the pasta. Return the chicken to the
skillet and reduce the heat to low. Cover and cook for 15 minutes or until
the chicken is cooked through and the pasta is tender but still firm.

Makes 4 servings

PREP: 5 MINUTES
COOK: 20 MINUTES

Easy Substitution Tip:

Substitute skim milk for the half-and-half.

Shrimp & Corn Chowder with Sun-Dried Tomatoes

1   can (10¾ ounces) Campbell's® Condensed Cream of Potato Soup
1½ cups half-and-half
2   cups whole kernel corn
2   tablespoons sun-dried tomatoes cut in strips
1   cup small **or** medium cooked shrimp
2   tablespoons chopped fresh chives
    Ground black **or** ground red pepper, optional

1. Heat the soup, half-and-half, corn and tomatoes in a 2-quart saucepan over medium heat to a boil. Reduce the heat to low. Cover and cook for 10 minutes.

2. Stir the shrimp into the saucepan. Sprinkle with chives. Cook until it's hot. Season to taste with black pepper, if desired.

Makes 4 servings

Shrimp Stuffing au Gratin

4½ cups Pepperidge Farm® Herb Seasoned Stuffing
3 tablespoons butter, melted
1¼ cups water
2 cups cooked broccoli flowerets
2 cups cooked medium shrimp
1 can (10¾ ounces) Campbell's® Condensed Cream of
   Mushroom Soup (Regular **or** 98% Fat Free)
½ cup milk
2 tablespoons diced pimiento (optional)
1 cup shredded Swiss cheese (4 ounces)

1. Coarsely crush **½ cup** of the stuffing. Mix with **1 tablespoon** of the butter in a small cup. Set aside.

2. Stir water and remaining butter in a 12×8×2-inch shallow baking dish. Add the remaining stuffing and stir lightly to coat.

3. Arrange the broccoli and shrimp over the stuffing.

4. Stir the soup, milk, pimiento and cheese in a small bowl. Pour the soup mixture over the shrimp mixture. Sprinkle with the reserved stuffing mixture.

5. Bake at 350°F. for 30 minutes or until hot.

Makes 6 servings

Campbell's Kitchen Tip:
You'll need to purchase 1 pound of fresh medium shrimp to have enough for 2 cups of cooked shrimp needed for this recipe. Heat 4 cups water in a 2-quart saucepan over high heat to a boil. Add the shrimp and cook for 1 to 3 minutes or until the shrimp turn pink. Drain in colander and rinse under cold water. Remove the shells and devein the shrimp, and it's ready to use.

PREP: 20 MINUTES
BAKE: 1 HOUR,
30 MINUTES

Time-Saving Tip:

To quickly peel the onions, put them in a medium bowl. Pour boiling water over them. Let stand for about 5 minutes. Drain and then slip off the skins.

Lemon-Basil Turkey with Roasted Vegetables

Vegetable cooking spray
2   medium lemons
    8-pound fresh turkey breast
24 baby Yukon Gold potatoes
1   butternut squash (about 1¼ pounds), peeled, seeded and cut into 1-inch cubes (about 3 cups)
8   medium beets, peeled and cut into 1-inch cubes (3¾ cups)
12 small white onions, peeled **or** 1 cup frozen small whole onions
1   tablespoon butter, melted
1   tablespoon dried basil leaves, crushed
1   cup Swanson® Chicken Broth (Regular, Natural Goodness™ **or** Certified Organic)

1. Spray a 17×11-inch roasting pan with cooking spray.

2. Cut **1** lemon into thin slices. Squeeze **2 tablespoons** juice from remaining lemon. Loosen skin on turkey breast and place lemon slices under the skin.

3. Place the turkey, meat-side up, potatoes, squash, beets and onions in the prepared pan. Brush the turkey with butter and sprinkle with basil. Insert a meat thermometer into the thickest part of the meat, making sure the thermometer is not touching the bone.

4. Stir the broth and lemon juice in a small bowl. Pour **half** of the broth mixture over the turkey and vegetables.

5. Roast the turkey at 375°F. for 1 hour. Stir the vegetables.

6. Add the remaining broth mixture to the pan. Roast for 30 minutes more or until the thermometer reaches 170°F.

Makes 8 servings

PREP: 15 MINUTES
BAKE: 50 MINUTES
STAND: 10 MINUTES

Vegetable Lasagna

2 cans (10¾ ounces **each**) Campbell's® Condensed Cream of Broccoli Soup (Regular **or** 98% Fat Free)
1½ cups milk
Vegetable cooking spray
1 tablespoon butter
3¾ cups sliced mushrooms (about 10 ounces)
2 medium red **or** orange peppers, cut into 2-inch-long thin strips (about 3 cups)
2 medium zucchini, thinly sliced (about 3 cups)
1 medium onion, thinly sliced (about ½ cup)
12 oven-ready lasagna noodles
2 cups shredded Monterey Jack cheese (8 ounces)

1. Stir the soup and milk with a whisk or spoon in a medium bowl. Set aside. Spray a 13×9×2-inch shallow baking dish with cooking spray.

2. Heat the butter in a 12-inch skillet over medium-high heat. Add the mushrooms, peppers, zucchini and onion and cook until the vegetables are tender.

3. Spread **1 cup** of the soup mixture in bottom of the prepared dish. Arrange **3** noodles and top with **one-third** of the vegetable mixture, **1 cup** of the soup mixture and **½ cup** of the cheese. Repeat the layers twice. Top with remaining noodles. Pour the remaining soup mixture over the noodles. Cover the dish with foil.

4. Bake at 375°F. for 40 minutes. Uncover and sprinkle with the remaining cheese. Bake for 10 minutes more or until hot. Let the lasagna stand for 10 minutes before serving.

Makes 8 servings

SAVORY SKILLET MEALS

When someone says "skillet meals," what do you think of? Meals that are hearty, easy to prepare and require almost no cleanup, we'll bet. These recipes make an entire meal in one pan, right on the stovetop.

Southwest Skillet

PREP/COOK: 25 MINUTES
STAND: 5 MINUTES

¾   pound ground beef
1   tablespoon chili powder
1   can (10¾ ounces) Campbell's® Condensed Beefy Mushroom Soup
¼   cup water
1   can (14½ ounces) whole peeled tomatoes, cut up
1   can (about 15 ounces) kidney beans, rinsed and drained
¾   cup **uncooked** instant white rice
½   cup shredded Cheddar cheese
    Tortilla chips

1. Cook the beef with chili powder in a 10-inch skillet over medium-high heat until it's well browned, stirring frequently to break up meat. Pour off any fat.

2. Stir the soup, water, tomatoes and beans into the skillet. Heat to a boil. Reduce the heat to low. Cover and cook for 10 minutes.

3. Stir in the rice. Cover the skillet and remove from the heat. Let stand for 5 minutes. Fluff the rice with a fork. Top with the cheese. Serve with the chips.

Makes 4 servings

Skillet Fiesta Chicken & Rice

1   tablespoon vegetable oil
4   skinless, boneless chicken breast halves
1   can (10¾ ounces) Campbell's® Condensed Tomato Soup
      (Regular **or** Healthy Request®)
1⅓ cups water
1   teaspoon chili powder
1½ cups **uncooked** instant white rice
¼   cup shredded Cheddar cheese

1. Heat the oil in a 10-inch skillet over medium-high heat. Add the chicken and cook for 10 minutes or until it's well browned on both sides. Remove the chicken and set aside. Pour off any fat.

2. Stir the soup, water and chili powder into the skillet. Heat to a boil.

3. Stir in the rice. Place the chicken on the rice mixture. Sprinkle chicken with additional chili powder and the cheese. Reduce the heat to low. Cover and cook for 5 minutes or until the chicken is cooked through and the rice is tender. Stir the rice mixture before serving.

Makes 4 servings

Honey Mustard Chicken

Did you know…?

Shredded or match-stick carrots are now available in bags in the produce section of many supermarkets. Substitute 1 cup for the carrots in the recipe.

2 tablespoons cornstarch

1¾ cups Swanson® Chicken Broth (Regular, Natural Goodness™ **or** Certified Organic)

1 tablespoon honey

1 tablespoon Dijon-style mustard

4 skinless, boneless chicken breast halves

1 large carrot, cut into 2-inch matchstick-thin strips (about 1 cup)

1 medium onion, sliced (about ½ cup)

Hot cooked rice, cooked without salt, optional

1. Stir the cornstarch, broth, honey and mustard in a small bowl. Set the mixture aside.

2. Cook the chicken in a nonstick 10-inch skillet over medium-high heat until it's well browned on both sides. Remove the chicken and set aside.

3. Add the carrot and onion to the skillet. Reduce the heat to low. Cover and cook for 5 minutes or until the vegetables are tender-crisp.

4. Stir the cornstarch mixture and stir it into the skillet. Cook and stir until mixture boils and thickens. Return the chicken to the skillet. Cover and cook for 5 minutes or until the chicken is cooked through. Serve with the rice, if desired.

Makes 4 servings

PREP: 5 MINUTES
COOK: 20 MINUTES

Lemon Broccoli Chicken

1   lemon
1   tablespoon vegetable oil
4   skinless, boneless chicken breast halves
1   can (10¾ ounces) Campbell's® Condensed Cream of Broccoli
      Soup (Regular **or** 98% Fat Free)
¼   cup milk
⅛   teaspoon ground black pepper

1. Cut **4** thin slices of lemon. Squeeze **2 teaspoons** juice from remaining lemon.

2. Heat the oil in a 10-inch skillet over medium-high heat. Add the chicken and cook for 10 minutes or until it's well browned on both sides. Remove the chicken and set aside.

3. Stir the soup, milk, lemon juice and black pepper into the skillet. Heat to a boil. Return the chicken to the skillet and reduce the heat to low. Top the chicken with the lemon slices. Cover and cook for 5 minutes or until the chicken is cooked through.

Makes 4 servings

61

PREP: 10 MINUTES
COOK: 15 MINUTES

Did you know…?

In the early days of the Campbell Soup Company, during tomato harvest season, the streets of Camden, New Jersey, would sometimes be red with tomatoes as they fell off the backs of delivery trucks and farm wagons en route to the plant. Their ultimate destination: Campbell's Condensed Tomato Soup.

Tomato Basil Chicken

1	tablespoon vegetable oil
6	skinless, boneless chicken breast halves
1	can (10¾ ounces) Campbell's® Condensed Tomato Soup (Regular **or** Healthy Request®)
½	cup milk
2	tablespoons grated Parmesan cheese
½	teaspoon dried basil leaves, crushed
¼	teaspoon garlic powder **or** 2 cloves garlic, minced
3	cups medium tube-shaped pasta (ziti), cooked and drained

1. Heat the oil in a 10-inch skillet over medium-high heat. Add the chicken and cook for 10 minutes or until it's well browned on both sides. Remove the chicken and set aside.

2. Stir the soup, milk, cheese, basil and garlic powder into the skillet. Heat to a boil. Return the chicken to the skillet and reduce the heat to low. Cover and cook for 5 minutes or until the chicken is cooked through.

3. Serve with the pasta.

Makes 6 servings

2-Bean Chili

1	pound ground beef
1	large green pepper, chopped (about 1 cup)
1	large onion, chopped (about 1 cup)
2	tablespoons chili powder
¼	teaspoon ground black pepper
3	cups Campbell's® Tomato Juice
1	can (about 15 ounces **each**) kidney beans **and** great Northern beans, rinsed and drained
	Sour cream, sliced green onions, shredded Cheddar cheese **and/or** chopped tomato (optional)

1. Cook the beef, green pepper, onion, chili powder and black pepper in a 10-inch skillet over medium-high heat until it's well browned, stirring frequently to break up meat. Pour off any fat.

2. Stir the tomato juice and beans into the skillet. Reduce the heat to low. Cook until the mixture is hot and bubbling. Top with sour cream, green onions, cheese and tomato, if desired.

Makes 6 servings

Autumn Pork Chops

 1 tablespoon vegetable oil
 4 bone-in pork chops, ½-inch thick
 1 can (10¾ ounces) Campbell's® Condensed Cream
     of Celery Soup (Regular **or** 98% Fat Free)
 ½ cup apple juice **or** water
 2 tablespoons spicy-brown mustard
 1 tablespoon honey
     Generous dash ground black pepper
     Hot cooked medium egg noodles

1. Heat the oil in a 10-inch skillet over medium-high heat. Add the pork chops and cook until the chops are well browned on both sides. Remove the pork chops and set aside.

2. Stir the soup, apple juice, mustard, honey and black pepper into the skillet. Heat to a boil. Return the pork chops to the skillet and reduce the heat to low. Cover and cook for 5 minutes or until the chops are cooked through but slightly pink in center.

3. Serve with the noodles.

Makes 4 servings

PREP/COOK: 15 MINUTES

Beefy Pasta Skillet

1   pound ground beef

1   medium onion, chopped (about ½ cup)

1   can (10¾ ounces) Campbell's® Condensed Tomato Soup (Regular **or** Healthy Request®)

¼   cup water

1   tablespoon Worcestershire sauce

½   cup shredded Cheddar cheese

1½   cups corkscrew-shaped pasta **or** 1 cup elbow macaroni, cooked and drained

1. Cook the beef and onion in a 10-inch skillet over medium-high heat until the beef is well browned, stirring frequently to break up meat. Pour off any fat.

2. Stir the soup, water, Worcestershire, cheese and pasta into the skillet. Cook and stir until the mixture is hot and bubbling.

Makes 4 servings

Cajun Fish

PREP: 5 MINUTES
COOK: 20 MINUTES

1 tablespoon vegetable oil

1 small green pepper, diced (about ⅔ cup)

½ teaspoon dried oregano leaves, crushed

1 can (10¾ ounces) Campbell's® Condensed Tomato Soup
(Regular **or** Healthy Request®)

⅓ cup water

⅛ teaspoon **each** garlic powder, ground black pepper **and**
ground red pepper

1 pound fresh **or** thawed frozen fish fillets*
Hot cooked rice, cooked without added salt

*Cod, haddock or halibut

1. Heat the oil in a 10-inch skillet over medium-high heat. Add the green pepper and oregano and cook until the green pepper is tender-crisp, stirring often.

2. Stir the soup, water, garlic powder, black pepper and red pepper into the skillet. Heat to a boil. Place the fish into the soup mixture and reduce the heat to low. Cover and cook for 5 minutes or until the fish flakes easily when tested with a fork. Serve with the rice.

Makes 4 servings

Did you know…?

Dr. John T. Dorrance, the first owner and president of Campbell Soup Company, grew tomatoes at his home in rural Cinnaminson, New Jersey, in an attempt to grow the perfect tomato for his soup. There is even a tomato variety named after him: the JTD.

PREP/COOK: 25 MINUTES

Country Skillet Supper

Did you know...?

Here's an easy way to peel garlic cloves: Separate the clove from the head, place it on a wooden chopping board and smash it with the flat side of a chef's knife or the bottom of a heavy glass. The peel will slip right off.

1   pound ground beef
1   medium onion, chopped (about ½ cup)
⅛   teaspoon garlic powder **or** 1 clove garlic, minced
1   can (10¾ ounces) Campbell's® Condensed Golden Mushroom Soup
1   can (10½ ounces) Campbell's® Condensed Beef Broth
½   teaspoon dried thyme leaves, crushed
1   can (14½ ounces) diced tomatoes
1   small zucchini, sliced (about 1 cup)
1½ cups **uncooked** corkscrew-shaped pasta

1. Cook the beef, onion and garlic powder in a 10-inch skillet over medium-high heat until the beef is well browned, stirring frequently to break up meat. Pour off any fat.

2. Stir the soup, broth, thyme, tomatoes and zucchini into the skillet. Heat to a boil. Stir in the pasta and reduce the heat to low. Cook and stir for 15 minutes or until the pasta is tender but still firm.

Makes 4 servings

Jambalaya One-Dish

PREP/COOK: 20 MINUTES

1 tablespoon vegetable oil

2 skinless, boneless chicken breasts, cut into cubes

½ pound hot Italian pork sausage, casing removed

¼ teaspoon garlic powder **or** 2 cloves garlic, minced

1 can (10½ ounces) Campbell's® Condensed French Onion Soup

⅓ cup Pace® Picante Sauce

1 cup **uncooked** instant white rice

½ pound frozen cooked large shrimp, shelled and deveined

½ cup frozen peas

Did you know…?

The Creole favorite, jambalaya, probably is taken from the French word for ham, jambon, which was a common ingredient in the first recipes for the dish.

1. Heat the oil in a 10-inch skillet over medium-high heat. Add the chicken, sausage and garlic and cook until the chicken and sausage are well browned, stirring often. Pour off any fat.

2. Stir the soup and picante sauce into the skillet. Heat to a boil. Stir in the rice, shrimp and peas and reduce the heat to low. Cover and cook for 5 minutes or until the chicken and sausage are cooked through and the rice is tender. Fluff the rice with a fork.

Makes 4 servings

PREP: 5 MINUTES
BAKE: 20 MINUTES

Mushroom Garlic Pork Chops

 1 tablespoon vegetable oil
 4 bone-in pork chops, ½-inch thick
 1 can (10¾ ounces) Campbell's® Condensed Cream of Mushroom with Roasted Garlic Soup
 ½ cup milk

1. Heat the oil in a 10-inch skillet over medium-high heat. Add the pork chops and cook until the chops are well browned on both sides. Remove the pork chops and set them aside.

2. Stir the soup and milk into the skillet. Heat to a boil. Return the pork chops to the skillet and reduce the heat to low. Cover and cook for 5 minutes or until the chops are cooked through but slightly pink in center.

Makes 4 servings

Quick Beef Skillet

1   pound ground beef

1   can (10¾ ounces) Campbell's® Condensed Beefy Mushroom Soup

¼ cup water

1   tablespoon Worcestershire sauce

⅛ teaspoon ground black pepper

1   can (about 15 ounces) sliced potatoes, drained

1   can (about 8 ounces) sliced carrots, drained

1. Cook the beef in a 10-inch skillet over medium-high heat until it's well browned, stirring frequently to break up meat. Pour off any fat.

2. Stir the soup, water, Worcestershire, black pepper, potatoes and carrots into the skillet. Cook and stir until the mixture is hot and bubbling.

Makes 4 servings

PREP: 10 MINUTES
COOK: 40 MINUTES

Pork Chop Skillet Dinner

1   tablespoon olive **or** vegetable oil
4   pork chops, ¾-inch thick
1   medium onion, chopped (about ½ cup)
1   cup **uncooked** regular long-grain white rice
1   can (10½ ounces) Campbell's® Condensed Chicken Broth
1   cup orange juice
3   tablespoons chopped fresh parsley
4   orange slices

1. Heat the oil in a 10-inch skillet over medium-high heat. Add the pork chops and cook until the chops are well browned on both sides. Remove the chops and set aside.

2. Add the onion and rice to the skillet. Cook until the rice is browned, stirring constantly.

3. Stir the broth, orange juice and **2 tablespoons** of the parsley into the skillet. Heat to a boil. Return the chops to the skillet and reduce the heat to low. Cover and cook for 20 minutes or until the pork is cooked through and the rice is tender. Top with the orange slices and sprinkle with the remaining parsley.

Makes 4 servings

PREP/COOK: 20 MINUTES

Shortcut Beef Stew

Easy Substitution Tip:

Substitute 5 cups frozen vegetables (carrots, small whole onions, cut green beans, cauliflower, zucchini, peas or lima beans) for the frozen vegetables for stew.

1 tablespoon vegetable oil

1 pound boneless beef sirloin steak, ¾-inch thick, cut into 1-inch pieces

1 can (10¾ ounces) Campbell's® Condensed Tomato Soup (Regular **or** Healthy Request®)

1 can (10½ ounces) Campbell's® Condensed French Onion Soup

1 tablespoon Worcestershire sauce

1 bag (24 ounces) frozen vegetables for stew (potatoes, carrots, celery)

1. Heat the oil in a 10-inch skillet over medium-high heat. Add the beef and cook until it's well browned, stirring often.

2. Stir the soups, Worcestershire and vegetables into the skillet. Heat to a boil. Reduce the heat to low. Cover and cook for 10 minutes or until the vegetables are tender.

Makes 4 servings

Shortcut Stroganoff

PREP/COOK: 20 MINUTES

1 tablespoon vegetable oil

1 pound boneless beef sirloin steak, cut into thin strips

1 can (10¾ ounces) Campbell's® Condensed Cream of Mushroom Soup (Regular **or** 98% Fat Free)

1 can (10½ ounces) Campbell's® Condensed Beef Broth

1 cup water

2 teaspoons Worcestershire sauce

3 cups **uncooked** corkscrew-shaped pasta

½ cup sour cream

Did you know…?

You should always add sour cream at the end of cooking, and don't let the mixture boil after adding it. Merely let it heat through. Because sour cream is a dairy product, it will curdle if it reaches the boiling point.

1. Heat the oil in a 10-inch skillet over medium-high heat. Add the beef and cook until it's well browned, stirring often.

2. Stir the soup, broth, water, Worcestershire and pasta into the skillet. Heat to a boil. Reduce the heat to medium. Cook and stir for 15 minutes or until the pasta is tender but still firm. Stir in the sour cream. Cook until the mixture is hot and bubbling.

Makes 4 servings

SLOW COOKING FAVORITES

Slow cookers have never been more popular and for good reason: They don't need tending, and slow-cooker meals don't require a lot of preparation. With these recipes, you literally pour in the ingredients, turn on the button and go. Dinner is ready and waiting when you get home.

Slow-Cooked Autumn Brisket

PREP: 20 MINUTES
COOK: 8 TO 9 HOURS

3-pound boneless beef brisket

1   small head cabbage (about 1 pound), cut into 8 wedges

1   large sweet potato (about ¾ pound), peeled and cut into 1-inch pieces

1   large onion, cut into 8 wedges

1   medium Granny Smith apple, cored and cut into 8 wedges

2   cans (10¾ ounces **each**) Campbell's® Condensed Cream of Celery Soup (Regular **or** 98% Fat Free)

1   cup water

2   teaspoons caraway seed (optional)

1. Season brisket if desired.

2. Put the brisket in a 6-quart slow cooker. Top with the cabbage, sweet potato, onion and apple.

3. Stir the soup, water and caraway, if desired, in a medium bowl. Pour the soup mixture over the brisket and vegetable mixture.

4. Cover and cook on LOW for 8 to 9 hours* or until the meat is fork-tender.

5. Remove the brisket from the cooker to a cutting board and let it stand for 10 minutes. Thinly slice brisket across the grain. Arrange brisket on a serving platter. Remove the vegetables and fruit with a slotted spoon and put on platter. Pour the pan juices into a gravy boat and serve with the brisket.

Makes 8 servings

*Or on HIGH for 4 to 5 hours

Did you know…?

Meat temperatures continue to rise for a few minutes after the meat is removed from the heat, so standing lets the meat finish cooking without drying out. Not only does this prevent overcooking, it also makes the meat easier to carve. Many experts also believe that standing permits the moisture in the meat, which comes to the surface during cooking, to return to the tissues, thereby making the meat moister.

PREP: 15 MINUTES
COOK: 7 TO 8 HOURS,
40 MINUTES

Jambalaya

2 cups Swanson® Chicken Broth (Regular, Natural Goodness™ **or** Certified Organic)

1 tablespoon Creole seasoning

1 large green pepper, diced (about 1⅓ cups)

1 large onion, diced (about 1 cup)

2 celery stalks, diced (about 1 cup)

1 can (about 14½ ounces) diced tomatoes

1 pound kielbasa, cut into cubes

¾ pound skinless, boneless chicken thighs, cut into cubes

1 cup **uncooked** regular long-grain white rice

½ pound fresh medium shrimp, shelled and deveined

1. Stir the broth, Creole seasoning, pepper, onion, celery, tomatoes, kielbasa, chicken and rice in a 3½- to 6-quart slow cooker.

2. Cover and cook on LOW for 7 to 8 hours*.

3. Stir the shrimp into the cooker. Cover and cook for 40 minutes more or until done.

Makes 6 servings

*Or on HIGH for 4 to 5 hours

Slow-Cooker Chicken & Dumplings

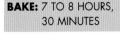

PREP: 20 MINUTES
BAKE: 7 TO 8 HOURS,
    30 MINUTES

2 medium Yukon Gold potatoes, cut into 1-inch pieces (about 2 cups)

2 cups fresh **or** frozen whole baby carrots

2 stalks celery, sliced (about 1 cup)

3 skinless, boneless chicken breasts, cut into 1-inch pieces

2 cans (10¾ ounces **each**) Campbell's® Condensed Cream of Chicken Soup (Regular **or** 98% Fat Free)

1 cup water

1 teaspoon dried thyme leaves, crushed

¼ teaspoon ground black pepper

2 cups all-purpose baking mix

⅔ cup milk

Did you know…?

For easy cleanup, spray the crock with nonstick cooking spray before adding the food. Or, try the new slow cooker liner bags.

1. Put the potatoes, carrots, celery and chicken in a 6-quart slow cooker.

2. Stir the soup, water, thyme and black pepper in a small bowl. Pour over the chicken and vegetables.

3. Cover and cook on LOW for 7 to 8 hours* or until the chicken is cooked through.

4. Stir the baking mix and milk until the ingredients are mixed. Spoon the batter over the chicken mixture. Turn the heat to HIGH. Tilt the lid to vent and cook for 30 minutes more or until the dumplings are cooked in the center.

Makes 8 servings

*Or on HIGH for 4 to 5 hours

PREP: 10 MINUTES
COOK: 8 TO 9 HOURS

Barley and Lentil Soup

8 cups Swanson® Beef Broth (Regular, Lower Sodium **or** Certified Organic)
2 cloves garlic, minced
1 teaspoon dried oregano leaves, crushed
4 large carrots, sliced (about 3 cups)
1 large onion, chopped (about 1 cup)
½ cup dried lentils
½ cup **uncooked** barley

1. Stir the broth, garlic, oregano, carrots, onion, lentils and barley in a 3½- to 6-quart slow cooker.

2. Cover and cook on LOW for 8 to 9 hours* or until the lentils and barley are tender.

Makes 8 servings

Or on HIGH for 4 to 5 hours

PREP: 10 MINUTES
COOK: 8 TO 10 HOURS

Did you know…?

The Joseph Campbell Preserve Company, the forerunner of Campbell Soup Company, chose red and white for its soup can labels in 1898, after company treasurer Heberton Williams attended a Penn-Cornell football game and was taken with Cornell's crisp red and white uniforms.

Coq au Vin

1	package (10 ounces) sliced mushrooms (about 4 cups)
1	bag (16 ounces) frozen small white onions (about 4 cups)
1	sprig fresh rosemary
2	to 2½ pounds skinless, boneless chicken (combination of thighs and breasts), cut into 1-inch strips
¼	cup cornstarch
1	can (10¾ ounces) Campbell's® Condensed Golden Mushroom Soup
1	cup Burgundy **or** other dry red wine
	Hot mashed **or** oven-roasted potatoes

1. Put the mushrooms, onions, rosemary and chicken in a 3½-quart slow cooker.

2. Stir the cornstarch, soup and wine in a small bowl. Pour the soup mixture over the chicken and vegetables.

3. Cover and cook on LOW for 8 to 10 hours* or until the chicken is cooked through. Remove rosemary sprig. Serve with potatoes.

Makes 6 servings

*Or on HIGH for 4 to 5 hours

PREP: 5 MINUTES
COOK: 7 TO 8 HOURS

Did you know…?

Slow cookers cook most efficiently when they're two-thirds to three-quarters full. That's because most slow cookers' heating units are coiled inside the outer walls that surround the crockery insert rather than just on the bottom of the crock, creating more even heat.

Golden Chicken with Noodles

2 cans (10¾ ounces **each**) Campbell's® Condensed Cream of Chicken Soup (Regular **or** 98% Fat Free)

½ cup water

¼ cup lemon juice

1 tablespoon Dijon-style mustard

1½ teaspoons garlic powder

8 large carrots, thickly sliced (about 6 cups)

8 skinless, boneless chicken breast halves

Hot cooked egg noodles

Chopped fresh parsley

1. Stir the soup, water, lemon juice, mustard, garlic powder and carrots in a 3½-quart slow cooker. Add the chicken and turn to coat with the soup mixture.

2. Cover and cook on LOW for 7 to 8 hours* or until the chicken is cooked through. Serve with the noodles. Sprinkle with the parsley.

Makes 8 servings

Or on HIGH 4 to 5 hours

PREP: 25 MINUTES
COOK: 7 TO 8 HOURS

Hearty Pork Stew

2 pounds sweet potatoes, peeled and cut into 2-inch pieces (about 2 cups)

2 pounds boneless pork shoulder, cut into 1-inch pieces

1 can (14½ ounces) Campbell's® Chicken Gravy

1 teaspoon dried thyme leaves, crushed

½ teaspoon crushed red pepper

1 can (15 ounces) black-eyed peas, rinsed and drained

1. Put the potatoes in a 4- to 6-quart slow cooker. Top with the pork.

2. Stir the gravy, thyme, red pepper and peas in a small bowl. Pour over the pork and potatoes.

3. Cover and cook on LOW for 7 to 8 hours* or until the meat is fork-tender.

Makes 8 servings

Or on HIGH for 4 to 5 hours

PREP: 10 MINUTES
COOK: 8 TO 10 HOURS

Did you know…?

There are few French food traditions as well known and respected as onion soup. The first owner and president of Campbell Soup Company, Dr. John T. Dorrance, wrote exacting standards and relied heavily on French cooking techniques for the company's soup creations.

Melt-in-Your-Mouth Short Ribs

    3   pounds beef short ribs, cut into individual pieces
    2   tablespoons packed brown sugar
    3   cloves garlic, minced
    1   teaspoon dried thyme leaves, crushed
   ¼   cup all-purpose flour
    1   can (10½ ounces) Campbell's® Condensed French Onion Soup
    1   bottle (12 fluid ounces) dark ale **or** beer
        Hot mashed potatoes **or** buttered noodles

1. Put the ribs, brown sugar, garlic and thyme in a 3½- to 6-quart slow cooker. Sprinkle with the flour and toss to coat.

2. Stir the soup and ale in a small bowl. Pour soup mixture over the ribs.

3. Cover and cook on LOW for 8 to 10 hours* or until the meat is fork-tender. Remove ribs with a fork or kitchen tongs from the sauce. Spoon off any fat from the sauce before serving. Serve with potatoes or noodles.

Makes 6 servings

*Or on HIGH for 4 to 5 hours

Brown Sugar Spice Cake

Vegetable cooking spray

1 can (10¾ ounces) Campbell's® Condensed Tomato Soup (Regular **or** Healthy Request®)

½ cup water

2 eggs

1 box (about 18 ounces) spice cake mix

1¼ cups hot water

¾ cup packed brown sugar

1 teaspoon ground cinnamon
   Vanilla ice cream

1. Spray the inside of a 3½- to 4-quart slow cooker with cooking spray.

2. Beat the soup, water, eggs and cake mix according to the package directions. Pour into the cooker.

3. Stir the water, brown sugar and cinnamon in a small bowl. Pour over the batter.

4. Cover and cook on HIGH for 2 to 2½ hours or until a toothpick inserted in the center comes out clean.

5. Spoon cake into bowls, scooping sauce from bottom of cooker. Serve warm with ice cream.

Makes 8 servings

Slow-Cooked Pulled Pork Sandwiches

PREP: 15 MINUTES
COOK: 8 TO 10 HOURS
STAND: 10 MINUTES

1 tablespoon vegetable oil
3½- to 4-pound boneless pork shoulder, netted or tied
1 can (10½ ounces) Campbell's® Condensed French Onion Soup
1 cup ketchup
¼ cup cider vinegar
3 tablespoons packed brown sugar
12 round sandwich rolls, split

1. Heat the oil in a 10-inch skillet over medium-high heat. Add the roast and cook until it's well browned on all sides.

2. Stir the soup, ketchup, vinegar and brown sugar in a 5-quart slow cooker. Add the roast and turn to coat with the soup mixture.

3. Cover and cook on LOW 8 to 10 hours* or until the meat is fork-tender.

4. Remove the roast from the cooker to a cutting board and let it stand for 10 minutes. Using 2 forks, shred the pork. Return the shredded pork to the cooker.

5. Divide the pork and sauce mixture among the rolls.

Makes 12 sandwiches
Or on HIGH 4 to 5 hours

Weekday Pot Roast & Vegetables

PREP: 15 MINUTES
COOK: 10 TO 12 HOURS
STAND: 10 MINUTES

2- to 2½-pound boneless beef bottom round **or** chuck pot roast
1   teaspoon garlic powder
1   tablespoon vegetable oil
4   medium potatoes (about 1 pound), each cut into 6 wedges
3   cups fresh **or** frozen baby carrots
1   medium onion, thickly sliced (about ¾ cup)
2   teaspoons dried basil leaves, crushed
2   cans (10¼ ounces **each**) Campbell's® Beef Gravy

1. Sprinkle all sides of roast with the garlic powder. Heat the oil in a 10-inch skillet over medium-high heat. Add the roast and cook until browned on all sides.

2. Put the potatoes, carrots and onion in a 3½-quart slow cooker. Sprinkle with the basil. Top with the roast. Pour the gravy over the roast and vegetables.

3. Cover and cook on LOW for 10 to 12 hours* or until the meat is fork-tender.

4. Remove the roast to a cutting board and let stand for 10 minutes before slicing. Serve the roast with the vegetables and gravy.

Makes 6 to 8 servings

*Or cook on HIGH for 5 to 6 hours

Did you know…?
You should keep a lid on it! The slow cooker can take as long as 20 minutes to regain the heat lost when the cover is removed. If the recipe calls for stirring or checking the dish near the end of the cooking time, replace the lid as quickly as you can. Otherwise, unless the recipe instructs you to remove the lid, don't, or food will take much longer to cook.

MAINSTAY MEALS

Every family has recipes they fall back on: meatloaf, pasta, roast chicken...the favorites that get them through the week. Here are some of our favorite "old standbys"—with their up-to-date variations—all in one chapter.

Best Ever Meatloaf

PREP: 10 MINUTES
BAKE: 1 HOUR,
          15 TO 30 MINUTES
STAND: 10 MINUTES

2 pounds ground beef
1 can (10¾ ounces) Campbell's® Condensed Cream of Mushroom Soup (Regular **or** 98% Fat Free)
½ cup fine dry bread crumbs
1 egg, beaten
1 small onion, finely chopped (about ¼ cup)
⅓ cup water

1. Thoroughly mix the beef, **½ cup** of the soup, bread crumbs, egg and onion in a large bowl. Put the mixture into a 13×9×2-inch baking pan and firmly shape into a 8×4-inch loaf.

2. Bake at 350°F. for 1 hour, 15 minutes to 1 hour, 30 minutes or until the meatloaf is cooked through. Remove the meatloaf with a slotted spatula to a cutting board. Let the meatloaf stand for 10 minutes before slicing.

3. Heat **1 tablespoon** of the pan drippings and the remaining soup and water in a 1-quart saucepan over medium-high heat to a boil. Serve with the meatloaf.

Makes 8 servings

Tried & True: Using soup in meatloaf has always been a popular way to add flavor to this family favorite. Our recipe for Best Ever Meatloaf has, over the years, called for Campbell's® Condensed Tomato Soup, Campbell's® Condensed Cream of Mushroom Soup, Campbell's® Onion Soup Mix and even combinations of soups. For a while, we loved to suggest using Campbell's® Condensed Vegetable Soup, so that kids would see letters when they cut into their dinner.

PREP: 10 MINUTES
COOK: 20 MINUTES

Broccoli & Noodles Supreme

3 cups **uncooked** medium egg noodles

2 cups broccoli flowerets

1 can (10¾ ounces) Campbell's® Condensed Cream of Chicken Soup (Regular **or** 98% Fat Free)

½ cup sour cream

⅓ cup grated Parmesan cheese

⅛ teaspoon ground black pepper

1. Prepare the noodles according to the package directions in a 4-quart saucepan. Add the broccoli during the last 5 minutes of the cooking time. Drain the noodles and broccoli well in a colander and return them to the saucepan.

2. Stir the soup, sour cream, cheese and black pepper into the noodles and broccoli. Cook and stir over medium heat until hot. Top with additional cheese before serving.

Makes 5 servings

Chicken & Roasted Garlic Risotto

PREP: 20 MINUTES
STAND: 5 MINUTES

4   skinless, boneless chicken breast halves
1   tablespoon butter
1   can (10¾ ounces) Campbell's® Condensed Cream of Chicken Soup (Regular **or** 98% Fat Free)
1   can (10¾ ounces) Campbell's® Condensed Cream of Mushroom with Roasted Garlic Soup
2   cups water
2   cups **uncooked** instant white rice
1   cup frozen peas and carrots

1. Season the chicken as desired.

2. Heat the butter in a 10-inch skillet over medium-high heat. Add the chicken and cook for 10 minutes or until it's well browned on both sides. Remove the chicken and set aside.

3. Stir the soups and water into the skillet. Heat to a boil. Stir in the rice and vegetables. Return chicken to the skillet and reduce the heat to low. Cover and cook for 5 minutes or until the chicken is cooked through. Remove from the heat. Fluff rice with a fork. Let stand for 5 minutes.

Makes 4 servings

Did you know…?
Traditional Italian risotto is made by cooking raw Arborio rice in a little butter then stirring hot stock into the rice a little at a time until the liquid is absorbed and the rice is soft and creamy. The creamy rice is then flavored with wine, herbs and cheese, and sometimes other ingredients, such as meat, fish or vegetables, are added.

Cavatelli with Sausage & Broccoli

Did you know…?

Until about the 1960s, the word "pasta" wasn't yet regularly used. Mostly, Americans ate either macaroni or spaghetti. This recipe calls for cavatelli— pasta shaped like little hot dog buns—that easily holds thick or chunky sauces.

1 package (16 ounces) frozen cavatelli pasta
1 tablespoon olive oil
1 pound sweet Italian pork sausage, casing removed
1 tablespoon butter
2 cloves garlic, minced
1 bag (about 16 ounces) frozen broccoli flowerets
1¾ cups Swanson® Chicken Broth (Regular, Natural Goodness™ **or** Certified Organic)
2 tablespoons grated Romano cheese
  Crushed red pepper

1. Prepare the pasta according to the package directions. Drain the pasta well in a colander. Return the pasta to the saucepot.

2. Heat the oil in a 10-inch skillet over medium-high heat. Add the sausage and cook for 8 minutes or until it's well browned, stirring frequently to break up meat. Remove the sausage with a slotted spoon and set aside.

3. Reduce the heat to medium and add the butter and garlic to the skillet. Cook and stir for 2 minutes or until the garlic is golden. Add the broccoli. Cook and stir for 5 minutes until tender-crisp.

4. Add the broth. Heat to a boil. Remove from the heat.

5. Stir the broccoli mixture, sausage and cheese to the saucepot. Cook over medium heat 10 minutes or until the sauce thickens, stirring occasionally. Serve with red pepper and additional cheese, if desired.

Makes 6 servings

PREP: 10 MINUTES
COOK: 20 MINUTES

Chicken Crunch

1 can (10¾ ounces) Campbell's® Condensed Cream of Chicken Soup (Regular **or** 98% Fat Free)
½ cup milk
4 skinless, boneless chicken breast halves
2 tablespoons all-purpose flour
1½ cups Pepperidge Farm® Herb Seasoned Stuffing, finely crushed
2 tablespoons butter, melted

1. Stir **⅓ cup** of the soup and **¼ cup** of the milk in a shallow dish. Lightly coat the chicken with the flour. Dip into the soup mixture. Coat with the stuffing.

2. Put the chicken on a baking sheet. Drizzle with the butter. Bake at 400°F. for 20 minutes or until the chicken is cooked through.

3. Heat the remaining soup and milk in a 1-quart saucepan over medium heat until hot, stirring occasionally. Serve the sauce with the chicken.

Makes 4 servings

Country Beef & Vegetables

1½ pounds ground beef
 1 can (26 ounces) Campbell's® Condensed Tomato Soup
 1 tablespoon Worcestershire sauce
 1 bag (16 ounces) frozen mixed vegetables
    Hot cooked rice
    Shredded Cheddar cheese

1. Cook the beef in a 10-inch skillet over medium-high heat until it's well browned, stirring frequently to break up meat. Pour off any fat.

2. Stir the soup, Worcestershire and vegetables into the skillet. Heat to a boil. Reduce the heat to low. Cover and cook for 5 minutes or until the vegetables are tender. Serve over the rice. Top with the cheese.

Makes 6 servings

Turkey Cutlets with Stuffing & Cranberry

Easy Substitution Tip:

If turkey cutlets are not available, purchase a whole turkey London broil (about 2 pounds) and cut it into 8 cutlets.

Make Ahead Tip:

Recipe can be prepared and fully cooked the day ahead. Refrigerate overnight. To reheat, cover and bake at 375°F. for 1 hour and 10 minutes or until hot.

1	bag (14 ounces) Pepperidge Farm® Cubed Herb Seasoned Stuffing
1	stick (½ cup) butter
1	stalk celery, chopped (about ½ cup)
1	medium onion, chopped (about ½ cup)
1¾	cups Swanson® Chicken Broth (Regular, Natural Goodness™ **or** Certified Organic)
1	can (16 ounces) whole cranberry sauce
8	turkey breast cutlets
1	can (10¾ ounces) Campbell's® Condensed Cream of Chicken Soup (Regular **or** 98% Fat Free)
⅓	cup milk

1. Crush **1 cup** of the stuffing to make coarse crumbs. Set aside.

2. Heat the butter in a 4-quart saucepan over medium heat. Add the celery and onion and cook until the vegetables are tender. Add the broth. Heat to a boil. Remove from the heat. Add the remaining stuffing and stir lightly to coat.

3. Put the stuffing mixture into a 13×9×2-inch baking pan. Spread the cranberry sauce over the stuffing. Top with the turkey.

4. Stir the soup and milk with a spoon in a small bowl. Pour evenly over the turkey. Sprinkle with the reserved stuffing crumbs.

5. Bake at 375°F. for 1 hour, 5 minutes or until the turkey is cooked through.

Makes 8 servings

PREP: 10 MINUTES
BAKE: 45 MINUTES

Easy Substitution Tip:
Substitute Campbell's®
Condensed Cream of
Broccoli Soup for the
Campbell's Condensed
Cream of Chicken Soup.

Lemon Chicken

1   lemon
1   tablespoon vegetable oil
    2½- to 3-pound whole broiler-fryer chicken, cut up
1   can (10¾ ounces) Campbell's® Condensed Cream of Chicken
    Soup (Regular **or** 98% Fat Free)
¼   cup water
1   clove garlic, minced
¼   teaspoon ground black pepper
    Hot cooked rice

1. Cut 4 thin slices from the lemon. Squeeze juice from the remaining lemon. Set aside.

2. Heat the oil in a 12-inch skillet over medium-high heat. Add the chicken and cook for 10 minutes or until it's well browned on both sides. Remove the chicken pieces as they brown. Pour off any fat.

3. Stir the soup, water, garlic, black pepper and reserved lemon juice into the skillet. Heat to a boil. Return the chicken to the skillet and reduce the heat to low. Cover and cook for 20 minutes.

4. Put the lemon slices on the chicken. Cover and cook for 15 minutes more or until the chicken is cooked through, stirring as needed to prevent sticking. Serve with the rice.

Makes 6 servings

Shortcut Chicken Cordon Bleu

1 tablespoon butter
4 skinless, boneless chicken breast halves
1 can (10¾ ounces) Campbell's® Condensed Cream of Chicken Soup (Regular **or** 98% Fat Free)
2 tablespoons water
2 tablespoons Chablis **or** other dry white wine
½ cup shredded Swiss cheese
½ cup chopped cooked ham
   Hot cooked medium egg noodles

1. Heat the butter in a 10-inch skillet over medium-high heat. Add the chicken and cook until it's well browned on both sides. Remove the chicken and set aside.

2. Stir the soup, water, wine, cheese and ham into the skillet. Heat to a boil. Return the chicken to the skillet and reduce the heat to low. Cover and cook for 5 minutes or until the chicken is cooked through. Serve with the noodles.

Makes 4 servings

PREP: 5 MINUTES
COOK: 25 MINUTES
STAND: 5 MINUTES

Did you know…?

By the 1970s, pasta was becoming more and more common on dinner tables as Americans began experimenting with international cuisines. Campbell Soup Company realized, though, that as American cooks got busier, many of them weren't making their own pasta sauces anymore; they were buying prepared sauce. So, in 1981, Campbell Soup Company introduced the Prego line, considered a premium brand in its category.

Skillet Chicken Parmesan

¼ cup grated Parmesan cheese

1½ cups Prego® Traditional Italian Sauce **or** Prego® Organic Tomato & Basil Italian Sauce

1 tablespoon olive oil

6 skinless, boneless chicken breast halves

1½ cups shredded part-skim mozzarella cheese (6 ounces)

1. Stir **3 tablespoons** of the Parmesan cheese into the pasta sauce.

2. Heat the oil in a 12-inch skillet over medium-high heat. Add the chicken and cook for 10 minutes or until it's well browned on both sides.

3. Pour the Italian sauce mixture into the skillet. Turn the chicken to coat with sauce. Reduce the heat to medium. Cover and cook for 10 minutes or until the chicken is cooked through.

4. Sprinkle the mozzarella cheese and the remaining Parmesan cheese over the chicken. Let stand for 5 minutes or until the cheese melts.

Makes 6 servings

Turkey & Broccoli Alfredo

PREP/COOK: 15 MINUTES

½ of a 16-ounce package linguine

1 cup fresh **or** frozen broccoli flowerets

1 can (10¾ ounces) Campbell's® Condensed Cream of Mushroom Soup (Regular **or** 98% Fat Free)

½ cup milk

½ cup grated Parmesan cheese

¼ teaspoon ground black pepper

2 cups cubed cooked turkey

Easy Substitution Tip:
Substitute spaghetti for the linguine and cooked chicken for the turkey.

1. Prepare the linguine according to the package directions in a 3-quart saucepan. Add the broccoli for the last 4 minutes of the cooking time. Drain the linguine and broccoli well in a colander. Return them to the saucepan.

2. Stir the soup, milk, cheese, black pepper and turkey into the linguine and broccoli. Heat, stirring occasionally until the mixture is hot and bubbling. Serve with additional cheese.

Makes 4 servings

TEMPTING
VEGETABLES
AND SIDES

Side dishes complement the main dish and round out your meal. Here's where you'll find Green Bean Casserole, Broth Simmered Rice, Moist & Savory Stuffing and so many of the dishes you depend on to make your meal complete and completely delicious.

Moist & Savory Stuffing

1¾ cups Swanson® Chicken Broth (Regular, Natural Goodness™
      or Certified Organic)
    Generous dash ground black pepper
1   stalk celery, coarsely chopped (about ½ cup)
1   small onion, coarsely chopped (about ¼ cup)
4   cups Pepperidge Farm® Herb Seasoned Stuffing

1. Heat the broth, black pepper, celery and onion in a 2-quart saucepan over high heat to a boil. Reduce the heat to low. Cover and cook for 5 minutes or until the vegetables are tender.

2. Add the stuffing and stir lightly to coat.

Makes 4 cups

Did you know...?
There really is a difference between stuffing and dressing. The ingredients can be the same, but if it goes inside the bird, it's stuffing. If it's baked in a baking dish or around the meat or bird, it's dressing.

Green Bean Casserole

PREP: 10 MINUTES
BAKE: 30 MINUTES

2 cans (10¾ ounces **each**) Campbell's® Condensed Cream of Mushroom Soup (Regular **or** 98% Fat Free)
1 cup milk
2 teaspoons soy sauce
¼ teaspoon ground black pepper
8 cups cooked cut green beans
1 can (6 ounces) French fried onions (2⅔ cups)

1. Stir the soup, milk, soy sauce, black pepper, green beans and **1⅓ cups** of the onions in a 3-quart casserole.

2. Bake at 350°F. for 25 minutes or until hot. Stir the green bean mixture.

3. Sprinkle the remaining onions over the green bean mixture. Bake for 5 minutes more or until onions are golden brown.

Makes 12 servings

Campbell's® Green Bean Casserole Trivia

• *Campbell's Condensed Cream of Mushroom Soup has been around for more than 70 years.*
• *Approximately 40% of all Campbell's Condensed Cream of Mushroom Soup ends up in a Green Bean Casserole.*

Tried & True: *The Green Bean Casserole, a perennial favorite at holiday dinners and potlucks across America, recently celebrated its 50th anniversary. This well-known and much-loved dish combines green beans, Campbell's Condensed Cream of Mushroom Soup, a splash of soy sauce (often considered the secret ingredient) and crunchy French fried onions. Created in 1955 by former Campbell's Kitchen manager Dorcas Reilly, it finds a place of honor on as many as 30 million holiday tables every year.*

A modest Reilly is still surprised that her original creation has become an American icon. She truly didn't realize just how popular the dish was until 10 years ago, during the 40th anniversary celebration. Dorcas Reilly was inducted into the Inventors Hall of Fame in 2002, and Campbell's Kitchen donated her now-yellowed 8×11-inch recipe test sheet to the National Inventors Hall of Fame Museum. She has been named the "Mother of the Green Bean Casserole."

"In the 1950s, we worked as a team to create recipes," she says. "We discussed ideas and had two taste testings each day in order to decide what worked and what didn't. Each recipe was scored on a scale of 1 to 5—we didn't talk or comment until all the scores were in. We reworked recipes and then tested again until we got it right."

"Our philosophy was to create winning combinations of ingredients that were quick and easy to put together and used staples most people had on hand. Our dishes had to look good, taste good, be easily made and economical—the Green Bean Casserole is the essence of all we wanted to accomplish when creating a new recipe."

Green beans are still one of America's favorite vegetables and the Green Bean Casserole will almost certainly be on holiday tables for years and years to come.

PREP/COOK: 25 MINUTES

Easy Substitution Tip:
Substitute Swanson®
Beef Broth or Vegetable
Broth or Seasoned Broths
for the Chicken Broth.

Broth Simmered Rice

1¾ cups Swanson® Chicken Broth (Regular, Natural Goodness™
   or Certified Organic)
 ¾ cup **uncooked** regular long-grain white rice

1. Heat the broth in a 2-quart saucepan over medium-high heat to a boil.

2. Stir in the rice. Reduce the heat to low. Cover the saucepan and cook for 20 minutes or until the rice is tender and most of the liquid is absorbed.

Makes 4 servings

Tried &True: *Cooking rice in Swanson broth instead of water will help you "bring your food alive," as our ad campaign so proudly stated in 1991. A concept as simple as substituting Swanson broth for water led to a recipe revolution and an ad campaign in which Campbell's Kitchen showed cooks how to step up the flavor of foods from rice to potatoes by cooking in broth instead of water.*

Cheddar Broccoli Bake

PREP: 10 MINUTES
BAKE: 30 MINUTES

1   can (10¾ ounces) Campbell's® Condensed Cheddar Cheese
    Soup
½   cup milk
    Dash ground black pepper
4   cups cooked broccoli cuts
1   can (2.8 ounces) French fried onions (1⅓ cups)

1. Stir the soup, milk, black pepper, broccoli and **⅔ cup** of the onions in a 1½-quart casserole. Cover the dish with foil.

2. Bake at 350°F. for 25 minutes or until hot. Uncover and stir the broccoli mixture.

3. Sprinkle the remaining onions over the broccoli mixture. Bake for 5 minutes more or until the onions are golden.

Makes 6 servings

PREP: 10 MINUTES
BAKE: 30 MINUTES

Easy Substitution Tip:
Substitute Campbell's®
Condensed Cream of
Mushroom Soup for the
Campbell's Condensed
Cheddar Cheese Soup
and chopped roasted
sweet peppers for the
green onion.

Cheddar Potato Bake

2	cups water
3	tablespoons butter
¾	cup milk
2	cups instant potato flakes **or** buds
1	can (10¾ ounces) Campbell's® Condensed Cheddar Cheese Soup
⅓	cup sour cream **or** plain yogurt
	Generous dash ground black pepper
1	medium green onion, chopped (about 2 tablespoons)

1. Heat the water and butter in a 2-quart saucepan over high heat to a boil. Remove from the heat. Stir in the milk. Slowly stir in the potatoes.

2. Stir the potatoes, soup, sour cream, black pepper and green onion in a 1½-quart casserole.

3. Bake at 350°F. for 30 minutes or until hot.

Makes 8 servings

Scalloped Potato-Onion Bake

PREP: 10 MINUTES
BAKE: 1 HOUR,
      30 MINUTES

1   can (10¾ ounces) Campbell's® Condensed Cream of Celery
      Soup (Regular **or** 98% Fat Free)
½   cup milk
      Dash ground black pepper
4   medium potatoes (about 1¼ pounds), thinly sliced
1   small onion, thinly sliced (about ¼ cup)
1   tablespoon butter, cut into pieces
      Paprika

Did you know…?

A scalloped vegetable is layered in a baking dish with a creamy sauce and then baked. Often bread-crumbs or other toppings are added before baking. Because Campbell's condensed cream soups can substitute for white sauce, scalloped vegetables are an easy side dish choice.

1. Stir the soup, milk and black pepper with a whisk or fork in a small bowl. Layer **half** of the potatoes, **half** of the onion and **half** of the soup mixture in a 1½-quart casserole. Repeat the layers. Place the butter over the soup mixture. Sprinkle with the paprika. Cover the dish with foil.

2. Bake at 400°F. for 1 hour. Uncover and bake for 15 minutes more or until the potatoes are fork-tender.

Makes 6 servings

Simmered Vegetables

PREP: 5 MINUTES
COOK: 15 MINUTES

1   can (10½ ounces) Campbell's® Condensed Chicken Broth
½   cup water
4   cups cut up fresh **or** 1 bag (20 ounces) frozen vegetable
      combination (broccoli, cauliflower, carrots)

Heat the broth, water and vegetables in a 2-quart saucepan over medium-high heat to a boil. Reduce the heat to low. Cover and cook for 5 minutes or until the vegetables are tender. Drain.

Makes 4 servings

PREP: 5 MINUTES
COOK: 20 MINUTES

Ultra Creamy Mashed Potatoes

3½ cups Swanson® Chicken Broth (Regular, Natural Goodness™ **or** Certified Organic)

5 large potatoes, cut into 1-inch pieces (about 7½ cups)

½ cup light cream

2 tablespoons butter
   Generous dash ground black pepper

1. Heat the broth and potatoes in a 3-quart saucepan over medium-high heat to a boil.

2. Reduce the heat to medium. Cover and cook for 10 minutes or until the potatoes are tender. Drain, reserving the broth.

3. Mash the potatoes with **¼ cup** of the broth, cream, butter and black pepper. Add additional broth, if needed, until desired consistency.

Makes about 6 servings

Tried & True: *Nutrition trends come and go, and recipes work hard to keep up. Campbell's Kitchen developed Skinny Mashed Potatoes in 1994, substituting Swanson broth for the traditional milk, cream and butter, successfully bringing down the fat content from 8 grams per serving to 0 grams. In 2002, though, consumers told us they sometimes missed the creaminess of traditional mashed potatoes, so we developed Ultra Creamy Mashed Potatoes—now there's a choice!*

Creamy Vegetable Medley

1   can (10¾ ounces) Campbell's® Condensed Cream of Celery
       Soup (Regular **or** 98% Fat Free)
½   cup milk
2   cups broccoli flowerets
2   medium carrots, sliced (about 1 cup)
1   cup cauliflower flowerets

Heat the soup, milk, broccoli, carrots and cauliflower in a 3-quart
saucepan over medium-high heat to a boil. Reduce the heat to low.
Cover and cook for 15 minutes or until the vegetables are tender.

Makes 6 servings

PREP: 5 MINUTES
BAKE: 45 MINUTES

Time-Saving Tip:
To thaw the vegetables,
cut off 1 corner of bag,
microwave on HIGH for
5 minutes.

Swiss Vegetable Bake

1 can (26 ounces) Campbell's® Condensed Cream of Chicken
    Soup
⅔ cup sour cream
½ teaspoon ground black pepper
2 bags (16 ounces **each**) frozen vegetable combination (broccoli,
    cauliflower, carrots), thawed
2 cups shredded Swiss cheese (8 ounces)
1 can (6 ounces) French fried onions (2⅔ cups)

1. Stir the soup, sour cream, black pepper, vegetables, **1½ cups** of the cheese and **1⅓ cups** of the onions in a 13×9×2-inch shallow baking dish. Cover the dish with foil.

2. Bake at 350°F. for 40 minutes or until the vegetables are tender. Stir the vegetable mixture.

3. Sprinkle the remaining cheese and remaining onions over the vegetable mixture. Bake for 5 minutes more or until the onions are golden brown.

Makes 8 servings

Country Scalloped Potatoes

PREP: 15 MINUTES
BAKE: 1 HOUR,
        10 MINUTES
STAND: 10 MINUTES

1 can (10¾ ounces) Campbell's® Condensed Cream of Celery Soup (Regular **or** 98% Fat Free)

1 can (10½ ounces) Campbell's® Chicken Gravy

1 cup milk

5 medium baking potatoes (about 1½ pounds), peeled and thinly sliced

1 small onion, thinly sliced (about ¼ cup)

2½ cups diced cooked ham (about ¾ pound)

1 cup shredded Cheddar cheese (4 ounces)

1. Stir the soup, gravy and milk with a fork or whisk in a small bowl. Layer **half** of the potatoes, onion, ham and soup mixture in a 13×9×2-inch shallow baking dish. Repeat the layers. Cover the dish with foil.

2. Bake at 375°F. for 40 minutes. Uncover the dish and bake for 25 minutes. Top with the cheese. Bake for 5 minutes more or until the potatoes are tender and cheese melts. Let the potatoes stand for 10 minutes before serving.

Makes 6 servings

TIMELESS
APPETIZERS,
SNACKS AND MORE

Since our first cookbook was published in 1910 (when just having a friend over for lunch necessitated china, silver and a starched linen tablecloth), Americans have become much less formal when they entertain. These entertaining recipes and snacks reflect that, too.

Tangy Baked Wings

PREP: 15 MINUTES
BAKE: 45 MINUTES

  1   pouch Campbell's® Dry Onion Soup and Recipe Mix
 ⅓ cup honey
  2   tablespoons spicy-brown mustard
18   chicken wings (about 3 pounds)

1. Stir the soup mix, honey and mustard with a spoon in a large bowl.

2. Cut the chicken wings at the joints into 54 pieces. Discard the tips or save for another use. Put the wings in the bowl. Toss to coat with the soup mixture. Place the wings on a large shallow-sided baking pan.

3. Bake at 400°F. for 45 minutes or until the wings are cooked through, turning halfway during cooking.

Makes 36 appetizers

Did you know…?

Buffalo wings are named after Buffalo, New York, the city of their birth. The recipe originated in a restaurant and bar there, where spicy chicken wings were served with celery sticks and blue cheese dip.

PREP/COOK: 15 MINUTES

Souper Sloppy Joes

1 pound ground beef
1 can (10¾ ounces) Campbell's® Condensed Tomato Soup
    (Regular **or** Healthy Request®)
¼ cup water
1 tablespoon prepared yellow mustard
6 hamburger rolls, split

1. Cook the beef in a 10-inch skillet over medium-high heat until the beef is well browned, stirring frequently to break up meat. Pour off any fat.

2. Stir the soup, water and mustard into the skillet. Cook and stir until the mixture is hot and bubbling.

3. Divide the beef mixture among the rolls.

Makes 6 sandwiches

PREP/COOK: 5 MINUTES

5-Minute Burrito Wraps

1   can (11¼ ounces) Campbell's® Condensed Fiesta Chili Beef
    Soup
6   flour tortillas (8-inch)
    Shredded Cheddar cheese

1. Spoon **2 tablespoons** of the soup down the center of each tortilla.
Top with cheese. Fold the sides of the tortilla over the filling and then fold
up the ends to enclose the filling.

2. Place the burritos seam-side down on a microwavable plate.
Microwave on HIGH for 2 minutes or until they're hot.

Makes 6 burritos

PREP/COOK: 10 MINUTES

Cheesy Broccoli Potato Topper

4   hot baked potatoes, split
1   cup cooked broccoli flowerets
1   can (10¾ ounces) Campbell's® Condensed Cheddar Cheese
    Soup

1. Place the potatoes on a microwavable plate. Fluff up the potatoes with a fork. Divide the broccoli among the potatoes.

2. Stir the soup in the can with a spoon until it's smooth. Spoon the soup over the filled potatoes. Microwave on HIGH for 4 minutes or until they're hot.

Makes 4 servings

Party Meatballs

1½ pounds ground beef
⅓ cup dry bread crumbs
1 egg, beaten
⅓ cup finely chopped onion
1 can (10¾ ounces) Campbell's® Condensed Golden Mushroom Soup
½ cup sour cream
¼ cup water
2 teaspoons Worcestershire sauce
    Chopped fresh parsley

Did you know…?
*The Campbell's®
Condensed Cream of
Mushroom Soup/ground
beef combination has
been the starting point for
many Campbell's Kitchen
recipes over the years.
Served over hot cooked
noodles, Party Meatballs
also would make a filling
and tasty dinner.*

1. Thoroughly mix the beef, bread crumbs, egg and onion in a large bowl. Shape the mixture firmly into 60 (1-inch) meatballs. Place the meatballs on a 15×10-inch baking pan.

2. Heat the broiler. Broil the meatballs with the top of the meatballs 4 inches from the heat for 5 minutes or until browned, turning halfway during cooking. Spoon off any fat.

3. Heat the soup, sour cream, water and Worcestershire in a 12-inch skillet over low heat.

4. Add the meatballs to the skillet. Cook and stir for 10 minutes or until hot and meatballs are cooked through. Do not let the mixture boil. Sprinkle with the parsley.

Makes 60 appetizers

PREP: 5 MINUTES
CHILL: 2 HOURS

Time-Saving Tip:
To soften cream cheese, remove from wrapper and place on a microwavable plate. Microwave on HIGH for 15 seconds.

Did you know…?
Pepperidge Farm was founded in 1937 by Margaret Rudkin. Her asthmatic son had special nutritional needs, and she couldn't find whole-wheat bread in supermarkets, so she started baking it herself. Soon there was such a demand for her bread by family and friends that she started a business she named after the Pepperidge trees that grew on her farm. Campbell Soup Company purchased her company in the early 1960s.

Shrimp Dip

1   package (8 ounces) cream cheese, softened
1   can (10¾ ounces) Campbell's® Condensed Cream
     of Shrimp Soup
½   teaspoon Louisiana-style hot sauce
¼   cup finely chopped celery
1   tablespoon finely chopped onion
     Assorted Pepperidge Farm® Crackers, chips **or** cut up
     fresh vegetables

1. Stir the cheese in a medium bowl until it's smooth. Stir in the soup, hot sauce, celery and onion.

2. Refrigerate the mixture for 2 hours or until the flavors are blended.

3. Serve with the crackers, chips or vegetables for dipping.

Makes 2¼ cups

Soft Tacos

PREP/COOK: 15 MINUTES
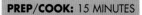

1 pound ground beef
1 package (1.12 ounces) Pace™ Taco Seasoning Mix
¾ cup water
8 flour tortillas (8-inch), warmed
1 cup Pace® Picante Sauce
1 cup shredded iceberg lettuce
1 cup shredded Cheddar cheese (4 ounces)

1. Cook the beef in a 10-inch skillet over medium-high heat until the beef is well browned, stirring frequently to break up meat. Pour off any fat.

2. Stir the taco seasoning mix and water into the skillet. Heat to a boil. Reduce the heat to low. Cook for 5 minutes.

3. Spoon about **¼ cup** beef mixture down center of each tortilla. Divide the picante sauce, lettuce and cheese among the tortillas. Fold the tortilla around the filling. Serve with additional picante sauce.

Makes 8 tacos

Did you know...?

"Picante" means "sharp, hot and spicy," in Spanish. Traditionally, Picante sauce is a Mexican red sauce made from chopped tomatoes, peppers and onions. David Pace, the inventor of Pace Picante Sauce in 1947, attended Tulane University on a football scholarship and played in the first Sugar Bowl.

Cheese Steak Pockets

1 tablespoon vegetable oil

1 medium onion, sliced (about ½ cup)

1 package (14 ounces) frozen beef **or** chicken sandwich steaks, separated into 8 portions

1 can (10¾ ounces) Campbell's® Condensed Cheddar Cheese Soup

1 jar (about 4½ ounces) sliced mushrooms, drained

4 pita breads (6-inch) cut in half, forming 8 pockets

1. Heat the oil in a 12-inch skillet over medium-high heat. Add the onion and cook until tender. Add the sandwich steaks and cook until they're well browned. Pour off any fat.

2. Stir the soup and mushrooms into the skillet. Cook and stir until the mixture is hot and bubbling.

3. Fill the pita halves with the meat mixture.

Makes 8 pita pocket sandwiches

Tomato Soup Spice Cake

PREP: 10 MINUTES
BAKE: 25 MINUTES

1   box (about 18 ounces) spice cake mix
1   can (10¾ ounces) Campbell's® Condensed Tomato Soup
    (Regular **or** Healthy Request®)
½   cup water
2   eggs
    Cream cheese frosting

1. Heat the oven to 350°F. Grease and lightly flour two 8- or 9-inch round cake pans.

2. Beat the cake mix, soup, water and eggs following the package directions. Spoon the batter evenly between the prepared pans.

3. Bake for 25 minutes or until a toothpick inserted in the center comes out clean.

4. Cool in pans on wire racks for 10 minutes. Remove the cakes from the pans and cool them completely on the wire racks.

5. Fill and frost the cake with your favorite cream cheese frosting.

Makes 12 servings

Tried & True: Soup in a cake? Why not? Campbell's® Tomato Soup Cake has been through many incarnations since it was first introduced: In 1940, Campbell's Kitchen developed Steamed Fruit and Nut Pudding. It was a classic steamed pudding made with, among other things, figs, raisins and nutmeats, spiced with cinnamon, nutmeg and cloves, and the secret ingredient, Campbell's Condensed Tomato Soup. Since then, soup cake has appeared as a sheet cake, cupcakes, layer cake and nut squares; in ginger and spice flavors; and as a traditional scratch cake and a cake mix. These days, the recipe calls for a spice cake mix, and we've created a version that can be baked in empty soup cans, making it a neat gift or table decoration—plus it's fun for kids.

Index